T0146674

God Threw Me Back

Me Back

A Child Survives War in Sudan

GATLUK G. DIGIEW

authorHOUSE®

AuthorHouse™
1663 Liberty Drive
Bloomington, IN 47403
www.authorhouse.com
Phone: 1 (800) 839-8640

Published by AuthorHouse 05/21/2018

ISBN: 978-1-5462-4245-1 (sc)
ISBN: 978-1-5462-4243-7 (hc)
ISBN: 978-1-5462-4244-4 (e)

Library of Congress Control Number: 2018905855

Print information available on the last page.

Any people depicted in stock imagery provided by Getty Images are models, and such images are being used for illustrative purposes only. Certain stock imagery © Getty Images.

This book is printed on acid-free paper.

Contents

Introduction

Everyone wants to know about my limp. Friends and even strangers ask, "What's wrong with your leg? Is it hurting you?" Most of the time, I just tell them I once was wounded. Some press further and ask if I have been shot. I just say, "Yes. I was shot," and leave it at that. Some people feel sorry for me. Some people try to imagine my pain and what I have gone through, but there is just no way they could understand being shot or living in war or even being a farmer's boy in rural South Sudan. I have never once told anyone the full story of that day I was shot—until now. Even my family does not know about the night I spent alone in the bushes, fighting to stay alive. For sixteen years, I have kept silent. I have tried to bury these memories—being conscripted as a boy soldier, war atrocities, survival tactics, life on the edge in refugee camps—to erase them from my mind, but I cannot. I thought that as long as I did not talk about that night and other horrors, everything would just vanish.

I know now there is no way to escape my past. Walking with a limp reminds me every day of my life where I am from and why I am here. Many refugees fear reprisals even decades after being resettled in a new country. I do not. It is time to share my story about my limp. It is time to speak for South Sudanese war victims, especially children, who are silent.

Prologue

A searing pain flashed in my hip. The bullet knocked me cold. My blood boiled hot. My body throbbed like all the drums in South Sudan beating at once.

I've been shot. Then, silence. Everything just stopped. Silence. I had not heard the gun, but I smelled the gunpowder. I heard people crying and screaming my name.

"Gatluk! Get up!" I tried to rise but fell. I tried again, but I could no longer feel my leg. Blood soaked my clothes, the ground, my hands. My friends and sister drew their arms over their skinny shoulders to try to carry me, but they were too small. I was already thirteen.

Now we could hear the Arabs yelling as they closed in on us. "Put me down! Go! Run!" I screamed. "If you stay, we all die. If you go, only one dies." With horrified eyes, they raced away.

Now I knew that my life was out of my hands. All I could do was wait for the militia to come finish me off. I heard their voices louder and louder. Nothing could stop them from killing me now. Strangely, this knowledge made me feel calm. I accepted that I would not escape death. I faced it. That army training when I was only nine rushed into my head: "Kill or be killed." Now it made sense.

Before the militias found me, I wanted to pray. I closed my eyes and said the first thing that came to mind: *Please Father, forgive them, for they know not what they do.*

Chapter 1

Growing Up: A Nuer Boyhood

I do not know when I was born. I have no birth certificate with my name because I was born in the family hut in Torpuot, South Sudan, not in a hospital. But I do know my family tree. For little boys in my Nuer culture, learning heritage is like learning the alphabet and was the first lesson my father taught me on the way to becoming a man. Somewhere between the ages of three and four, I started sitting in the barn of our compound with the men of the village and began to learn basic Nuer tradition. I learned that *Gat* means "son of" and *Nya* means "daughter of." It is important for a man to know his bloodline and his clan. Not knowing one's family tree means losing one's true identity, so I learned mine—Gatluk, Gatluak, Digiew Tut, Jauol—all my lineage, so I could pass it on to my children. In this way, my family would never end.

When I was five years old, my father began to teach me about things important in a man's life, just as he had taught my elder siblings. He would ask me questions to check my knowledge whenever we did something he knew was important. For example, when I was drinking milk, he taught me about cows.

"Milk is good, right?" he asked.

"Yes," I replied. "Milk is good."

"Where does milk come from?"

"It comes from a cow."

"So if milk is good and comes from a cow, then a cow is good, right?"

I nodded.

He went on. "When food is scarce, cows provide milk. When you are

1

looking for a woman, cows are a sign of wealth. And when there is reason for people to run away, cows will run on their own. You do not have to carry them."

My father made sure that I recognized the value of a cow at an early age because where I come from, cows are a measure of wealth. A man with many cows has everything and will risk his life to protect those cows, whether he must fight another man or a lion.

He also taught me that the greatest expectation for any Nuer boy is to grow up to be a strong man who can provide for his family. His lessons were his legacy to me, because where I come from, boys do not go to school. My village, Torpuot, is ten miles—about a day's walk—from the nearest school in Kuanylualthuan. We do not have cars. Instead of going to bed excited for school, I woke up each morning looking forward to my job taking care of the animals. My teachers were my father and other men in our village.

My father, Gatluak Digiew Tut, also known as Gatdigiew or son of Digiew, worked hard for us and made sure we always had food on the table. He did not talk a lot, but he was very easygoing. Like many fathers in South Sudan, he was a farmer, and my mother nicknamed him *Nguanthaak,* or Many-Ox. Our home compound in the open grassland had three round huts with thatched roofs and a barn for our animals: 65 cows, 140 sheep, and 40 goats. These provided milk, cheese, and meat. We labored the way our people had for centuries, with no machinery, like plows, or work animals. With just hand tools and axes, we cleared black land the size of two football fields and grew corn, sorghum, beans, pumpkin, and millet.

The stronger you were, the bigger your farm. The more sons you had, the better off you were. My father had five sons, Duol, Tut, Ngut, Gatdet, and me, enough manpower for another small tobacco farm. As a boy, I spent most days herding goats, sheep, and calves. My tasks included collecting cow manure with my bare hands. This never bothered me. It was just something I was expected to do.

One day, I nearly cut the finger off my little four-year-old brother as we tried to help Dad fix the barn. A hyena had clawed open the back of the barn during the night, trying to eat the goats and sheep. So little Gatdet and I helped Dad dig a posthole with choppers—sharp hoes—to support the wooden frames and then daubed mud to seal it. While we chopped the hard ground, Gatdet reached in to scoop dirt with his hands. I didn't see him in time and accidentally gashed his thumb. I was so mad at myself for causing my little brother so much pain I refused to eat for the rest of the day. I blamed my error on the hyena for putting us in that situation, for if the barn had not needed repairs, my brother's fingers would not have been near the chopper.

The hyena reminded me of the story old men used to tell of how God divided the elements. According to the story, God asked lion, hyena, bird, man, and dog what each one wanted. Lion took the cow, bird took the grain, hyena took the sheep, and dog took fire. There was nothing left for man except water. The others had completely forgotten about water, though they had received what they wanted. Man felt that he was left with nothing. When man asked God what was left for him, God looked around and told man to take water. Man protested and argued that he had nothing to eat. He was mad at God.

God called man over and showed him how foolish he was for ignoring the fish in the water. God showed him how to fish for food and reminded him that no one can live long without water. By this time, the others had gone their own way, and man was left sitting by the water. Not a day passed before the others came back, one by one, asking man for water. Man was guarding his water and would not allow anyone to drink without permission.

"You see," he told each of them, "God gave each of us what we wanted, and the water is now mine. If I let you drink my water, you must give me something in return." Because no one can survive without water, each animal gave man something in exchange—and man ended up with everything. That is why birds eat grain, dogs sleep by the fire, and shy men and lions fight over cows. When hyena gave man his sheep, he promised man he would be back for them. That is why the hyena tore open the wall of our barn, to take back what he felt was his.

*****

Men and women have very different responsibilities within a family in Nuer society. Because there is so much to learn before adulthood, girls are expected to stay among the women to learn how to cook, and the boys stay with the men to learn how to become good farmers. Anyone who did not adhere to these established gender roles was ridiculed. As soon as they were weaned and walking, boys always sat with men and girls with the women. We ate meals separately, too. If I were to sit next to a female, the men would call me all kinds of names like "man-lady" or "ass house."

My mother, Nyalam Kun Chol, encouraged me to be strong, even though I was next to the youngest. My name, Gatluk, means "baby judge"; she nicknamed me Lukmaan or Woman-Judge. All of us have nicknames. Thin and six feet tall, Mom has a big heart and treats everyone equally and with respect. No wonder she has so many friends and has never met anyone she did not like. She is known for her kindness and generosity and always offers guests food. I have yet to find anyone who cooks like her, especially her couscous. I am not ashamed to say I want to marry a girl just like my mother.

Even as very young boys, we were taught to ignore pain so we would not appear weak. Men do not cry where I come from because crying is a sign of weakness. People constantly reminded me to endure as much pain as possible. I should be fearless, they said. If a child fell and cried, male children would be pressured: "Are you a woman? Why are you crying?" Even if I tripped and tore loose a toenail, I would not cry. We were expected to show no emotion. We had to remain calm during every conversation, no matter how angry or upset we were. We must never cry.

Nuer society has another expectation for boys: the manhood ceremony. The age for becoming a man is around thirteen to fifteen, or as young as ten if the boy is tall. During this coming-of-age ritual, each boy must have six lines, *gaar,* cut by knife from ear to ear on his forehead to become a man. Boys have to be brave because if they cry, they bring shame on themselves and their families.

Weeks before the cutting took place, alcohol would be made and the person to perform the cutting found. He was an expert who might come from a different village. If he did not live close by, we would walk days to find him. He would then travel to our village and be paid with money or goat.

The night before the cutting in 1996 at the age of fifteen, my group of seven young men spent the night together. Parents and friends stopped by to encourage us. We were nervous and scared but, of course, showed no emotion. On the day of the cutting, a bull calf was sacrificed. Villagers didn't have to be invited; they knew and came. The feasting and singing would last all day.

The cutting was done at sunrise during the cool of the morning so we wouldn't bleed a lot. When it was time for the actual cutting, everyone sat and watched. I lay on the ground and positioned my head in a circular pillow of ashes. This steadied my head and caught the blood. If I flinched, the mark would not be straight and would prove forever that I was a coward. Because I did not wince, my lines were marked well and straight. The cutting took less than two minutes, and I didn't bleed too much. It hurt a little afterward; then I just healed.

Those six marks would identify you as a Nuer man within Nuer society or from other tribes. Each has a different meaning which must be honored by any Nuer man who received them. They are laws cut deep in your forehead to remind you every day in your life. The first line indicates that you are now a man and no longer a boy. Therefore, you must behave as an adult from that time onward. The second line means that you will not fear anything or any man, and that people must look up to you. The third line defines that you are now a warrior and that you will die fighting to protect your community from any threats or harm. You must never bring any disgrace to your family, because you are now consider a respectful leader and you will talk, behave, and carry yourself well in Nuer society. And you are now equal and can speak your mind freely like all Nuer men who came before with respect to your elders. The fourth line indicates that you shall not just eat everywhere. This mark requires you to have high self-respect and be an honorable person. The fifth line means that you must not be self-indulgent, acquisitive, or desirous. Therefore, you shall be among your peers and eat together. You may share and give a hand to others in time of need. And the sixth line outlaws sleeping with a married woman. The most important part about line six is that it is prohibited and a death sentence to have intimate relationship with any of your blood relatives. It would be necessary that one of you would die. If a child is born, the child would not be normal mentally or physically. Those are the laws and customs written on my forehead to guide me and live my life as a Nuer man.

But I felt different. I felt a new responsibility on my shoulders because now I had six scars on my forehead that proved I was a man. Now I had to act differently because I was expected to contribute to my Nuer community to protect the lives of everyone. This is the only way to enter manhood, and every boy goes through it. Now I was recognized as being strong enough to protect my village and my family. Now I could go to war. Now I was a man.

Secure within my family and village, I tended the animals as South Sudanese had for hundreds of years. My family attended a big Christian church of wood, mud, and grass that could seat about two hundred. I sang in the choir and learned the words by heart because I could not read. I became a drummer and my sister, the lead singer. Life was slow, simple, and predictable. Then one day, when I was about nine years old, my world broke apart and I could never put the pieces together again.

Chapter 2

I Learn About War

Before the second civil war in 1983, my parents would tell us stories about "Arabs," people who attacked villages, huts, barns, and churches and set them on fire. I had never seen an Arab. In fact, I had never seen anyone with skin a different color than mine. Even when my mother went to the Arab town of Nasir, called Kuanylualthuan, we children thought less about Arabs and more about the hard, round candies—yellow, red, and white— that she bought there. We ate them slowly so the sweetness would last.

My mother told a story about the day an Arab "helicopter," a flying machine, landed on the edge of the river in the cattle camp. Three men carrying metal cans jumped out of the helicopter and ran straight down to the river, where children were playing. When they reached the water, the men emptied their containers into the river; then they ran back to the helicopter and flew away. No one knew what they had poured into the water, but my mother said that a few days later, many of the people who had been in that water became very sick to their stomachs.

My mother also told about her uncle, who was killed when the Arabs dropped a bomb on his village. He had been working in the field behind his compound clearing wheat in a cornfield when the Arab helicopter came from nowhere and dropped the bomb that killed him. Though I did not know what a helicopter was, one thing I knew for sure was that these "Arabs" were nothing like my Nuer people I knew and trusted.

Even with Sudanese Arabs attacking villages, it was not until the Sudan People's Liberation Army/Movement (SPLA/M) formed in 1983 that life became frightening and the word *Arab* a word for terror. The

South Sudanese established the SPLA to fight injustices and inequalities that resulted when the northern Khartoum government denied South Sudanese basic human rights. The north imposed Islamic law on all of Sudan: Islam would now be the only religion practiced in all Sudan. Christians were converted by force. At this point, many schools that had taught English changed to Arabic. Non-Muslim children were forced to learn and memorize the Quran. Years later, I would meet a South Sudanese student who told how he had dug a hole to escape his classroom because he did not want to learn and memorize the Quran. He was quickly caught and beaten. Being Christian in Sudan at that time was like having a death sentence hanging over my family and me. Yet I knew that my family and other Christian families in my village would rather die than convert to Islam.

The newly formed SPLA grew in strength and numbers. Soldiers moved on foot, sweeping from village to village and through the jungles to recruit young men to their ranks. They thought nothing of forcing young boys and girls to carry bags of clothing, food supplies, and ammunition.

I remember the day the army came through my village when I was only six years old. A soldier made me carry his boots to the next village.

"Hey, you, *Jesh-Ameer.* Come here!" He used the Arabic word meaning *Red Army,* for young boys. My friend Chuol and I and other friends looked around nervously.

"Hey, you! Come here!" The soldier pointed right at me. I timidly approached, and he grabbed my left hand hard, pulling me toward him. His face looked so angry I thought he would slap me. He took three pairs of men's boots tied together by the laces and slung them over my left shoulder and heaped two AK-47 magazines with about sixty bullets in my arms. Then he pushed me in front of him and made me walk. The soldiers walked fast, and I could not keep up with them due to the weight of the boots and ammunition, about twenty to twenty-five pounds. Every time I slowed down, he screamed, "Move it!" I walked as fast as I could in my bare feet. I would not give the soldier any reason to beat me. When we reached the next village and he found another boy to take over my task, I was sent back to my village.

Even before I followed the trail two miles home, news had spread to my parents that the army had taken me. My dad sat in the shadow of our home when I arrived. I sat down beside him. He knew I was thirsty from the walk and handed me his clay water jug.

"Is it true, Gatluk that the army took you?"

"Yes. I was playing *Nya Goonya* (hopscotch) with Chuol and my other friends when one of the army men called me over. He told me to carry his boots."

"How far did you go with the army, then?" When I told him, he was not worried about the distance. He knew that the army would not hurt me, just as he knew that this was not the first time the army used boys to carry their supplies. With that, our conversation was over, and he went back to making *dap,* rawhide rope made from cow skin.

One day in early spring, about a month after the boot incident, my mother was sweeping the front of her hut and Dad sat repairing *dap* when I heard a louder and louder pounding noise but could not see anything. Then something a thousand times bigger than a bird roared over my village. I stood awestruck, trying to watch. I did not know that this giant bird with awesome sound was hunting for my family and me.

Mom grabbed my hand and dragged me under the palm tree. "Stay here!" She warned my older brothers, hoping it would be harder for the helicopter to spot us there. I saw fear in her eyes as she held little Gatdet and me so tight. She knew it had come to bomb us.

This big bird, this helicopter, confidently circled over our village. Before it could drop any bombs, the SPLA shot it. Suddenly, the helicopter spun in the air with black smoke spewing from the tail. When it crashed, the ground shook like very loud thunder. Then came smaller explosions like fireworks, lasting a few seconds. The SPLA men shouted for joy because it was the first time they had successfully shot down an Arab helicopter. There were no survivors.

My mom let go of our hands, and we came out from under the palm tree. I still could not understand what had happened. Mom went back to sweeping, my dad to mending *dap.* My brothers returned to preparing the evening fire with cow dung. Life returned to normal, but not for long.

About two hours after the first helicopter was gunned down, a second helicopter appeared. "Run under the tree, kids!" Mom yelled. We obeyed, but I still did not understand the danger. Over the village it flew, surveying the crash site. The SPLA shot again and again. Now the second helicopter crashed, this one into the lake. I thanked God for bringing the SPLA to our village. I believe that God did His miracle work that day. It could have been our last day alive, but God did not call us to be with Him that day. Not yet.

The following day, Arab army trucks rumbled through our village, shooting in all directions. Every few seconds, I heard, *boom,* another hand grenade and bursts of machine gun fire. The air filled with smoke and dust on all sides from the exploding rocket-propelled grenades (RPG) hitting barns and huts and setting them aflame as we fled our compound to run to the bushes.

For the first time, I felt confused and scared by what was happening to my home. Terrible noises, fires, and smells filled my ears and heart. Where was my peaceful home where cows mooed and birds chirped in the treetops? Where were the young men singing behind their herds in the evening hours and boys whistling behind their calves as they chased them home at dusk?

Suddenly, we saw people from the neighboring villages run toward us, screaming in horror. A few dozen became a stampede of hundreds, running, running, as smoke of their burning villages billowed behind them. The Arabs had attacked their villages first and set every house and barn on fire before they moved toward us. The SPLA ran to help the burning villages about three miles away, but our soldiers were outnumbered about five to one. Little could be done to slow the well-supplied Arab attack. Now it was every man for himself.

I stood frozen in fear. My sister grabbed my small hand, and my mother clasped my baby brother over her shoulder. We raced toward the woods half a mile away, stumbling and panting. We never looked back. Once in the bushes, we joined some of our relatives, but not my dad and brothers. They had run toward the cow pastures. The popping machine gun fire warned us it was not safe to look for them yet.

Against the clear blue skies above the trees, we watched smoke rise from our smoldering homes. Day faded into night. Babies cried. Huddled in groups, mothers tried to shush them. Even snuggled between my sister and mother, I could not sleep. I was scared that wild hyenas and lions might attack us. Still, the babies cried, but with nothing to feed them, there was nothing the mothers could do.

The next morning, my people began to search for relatives. Anguished crying in the woods meant someone had found a fallen loved one. People cried violently, throwing themselves on the ground and on top of their killed family members. Some held up the head of the body in shock, refusing to believe the person was dead. This first experience seeing a dead person filled me with terror and sadness. I wanted to cry, but knew I must not. Anger took over my emotions. All I could do was listen and watch.

We still had no word from my father and brothers, and we screamed for them in all directions. Finally, we found a man who had run with them to the pastures. He assured us they were fine and told us where to find them.

As soon as we found them, Dad spat on my head, a loving greeting, and I clung to his leg. Now that my family was reunited with my father and brothers, I felt safe. Our village and home had been reduced to ashes and memories, but no one in our family had been hurt or killed. Other families were not so fortunate and began to bury their dead behind their burned compounds. We were lucky to still have our livestock for milk, but my mother walked to my aunt's village to find food.

My six-year-old mind could not grasp all that had happened, but I could tell by my parents' voices and body language that they were afraid. Even so, they were determined to stay in the place they called home and to rebuild with other families who did not want to leave. Many families did move away, including many of my friends like Deng and Nhial. Losing Chuol was hardest of all. I would not see him again for twenty years.

Within six months, the SPLA had regrouped and attacked the Arab base on the Ethiopian border, a two-days' walk from us. The SPLA continued to increase its numbers by forcing some men from the villages to join its ranks and recruiting those who volunteered. In 1986, it returned to my village on its way to attack Nasir. I wondered what would happen. Would the Arabs send helicopters to bomb the SPLA in our village or send tanks to chase everyone out like they always did?

The SPLA did not waste time, and within a week of their arrival, the fight with the Arabs began. During night fighting, bullets like fireworks crisscrossed the sky in flashes of red, green, and white. We were afraid, so we slept at my relatives' village further from Nasir. When we returned to our village the next morning, we saw helicopters drop bombs on nearby villages.

These raids usually happened on Sundays because the Arabs knew the Christians would be gathered to pray. Churches became prime targets. Sometimes a man would stand guard outside the church to watch for incoming helicopters. When he signaled, we would run out of the church in case it was about to be bombed; but that was not the only threat. The Arabs dropped barrels filled with explosives, bombs, and poison gas on our villages. When my younger brother, Gatdet, got sick from the poison gas, my dad decided it was safer to go to his sister's village, a full day of walking away.

*****

Within a few months of attacking Nasir, the SPLA was forced to regroup once again. Too many of its ranks had been killed and too many resources had been depleted to continue to fight the Arab army. The SPLA retreated to the Ethiopian border to hide deep in the jungle where the Arabs couldn't find them.

Meanwhile, we continued to live at my aunt's village, where our family began to build new huts. Building a hut takes months, depending on the size and the number of people helping. The process required contributions from every family member, relatives, and friends.

First, my dad and my three older brothers began to gather wood from the forest to form the wall and the materials to tighten it. Mom, my sister, and I would carry the wood to the compound. There Dad would draw three circles in the ground the size of the huts to be made. Next, Dad and my brothers would dig a trench eighteen inches deep and two inches wide along the line of the circle for the foundation of the walls. While they dug the trenches, Mom, my sister, and I were busy collecting dirt, which would be used to seal the inside of the wooden walls. After the trenches were dug, the wood stakes were packed in upright and tied tightly together with *rok*, a rope. These sticks formed the walls of the huts. To complete the walls, we smoothed on mud, which would dry and block out the rain. My aunt's family helped us to collect water from a nearby pond to mix the mud and chopped grasses we had gathered earlier. Working together, we finished the inside walls of the three huts in one day. If my family had worked alone, this task would have taken a full week.

One week after the walls were finished, Dad and my brothers began to construct the roof framework from wood and rope. This was covered with long, dried grasses thick enough to withstand heavy rains. Mom began covering the first roof as soon as it was framed and worked long hours every day, often not stopping until after dark. Within six and one-half weeks, Mom completed the roofs of our three huts.

While Mom worked on the roof, my dad and my brothers started to cut down some trees with an ax to clear land the size of two and one-half football fields to plant crops. All the trees and limbs were left to dry for six weeks; then my father would set it on fire to clear all the brush and wheat seeds and to soften the soil. In three months, they completed preparing the field and waited for the rains to come. This was just the beginning of our work.

By June and the beginning of the rainy season, we had been in my aunt's village for seven months, completely surviving on food my aunt provided. Now my dad and brothers began to plant corn crops and tilled the field to keep it free from wheat. God blessed us that year with good rain, and our field produced enough food to feed my family for a whole year.

We felt safer here, except by now my kid brother, Gatdet was seriously ill.

Chapter 3

I Am Not a Big Brother Anymore

Little Gatdet struggled to breathe through lungs burned by the poisoned gas. We watched helplessly, for we had no access to doctors or medicine. My mother just sat by his side, day and night, helpless and praying to God to heal her sick child. I sat by and held his hand. Once we tried to play *gakalaklak,* a tickling game. I would try to make him laugh by tickling his arm, starting at his wrist and working up to his underarm. My game made Gatdet smile, but laughing hurt him too much.

Gatdet was so much more to me than just my little brother. He was also my best friend. I missed how we used to play together and the times we picked wild fruits like dates. Every time a fruit was out of his reach, he would call me to get it for him. Now as I looked at this gasping boy, I missed the little brother I used to know. I kept trying to convince myself that everything would be all right, but Gatdet was not getting any better. As much as I did not want to believe it, my little brother was slipping away from us.

Very soon it was Christmastime. My sister and I made the six-hour walk to our church for the Christmas celebration, but my parents did not join us. They stayed with Gatdet, who was far too sick to travel. At church, I played drums, something I had learned at our old compound on drum sets made by my father. Both my sister and I sang Nuer songs in the choir:

Jesus Kurei riew buay do waar lamber kuoth chi ben ka goy
hoa chi buom chiang nhial ro nyuoth nhaong do ka ko relaro

Jesus Christ, your purity brightens the darkness. You are a light of our heavenly father, you came for peace on earth. The power of heaven is shown, and your love to us is unique.

Another song we used to sing was this:

Gat kuoth Nhial ni Yecu, chu ko kuon chaangda changka kon ji duari

Jesus, son of heavenly Christ, do not forsake us, our creator, even though we are sinners.

Three days later, when we returned to our compound from the celebration, I saw Dad sitting with his head between his knees and Mom sitting against the wall of the hut with her legs out in front of her. They were so still I knew something was wrong. I called out, but no one answered. I could tell my mother had been crying, and her skin was dry and pale. When Dad looked up, I was startled to see how emotionally broken he was. He may have cried that day.

Suddenly, I needed to find Gatdet. I ran inside the hut but could not find my brother.

"Mom! Where is Gatdet? Where is Gatdet, Mom?" My voice shook, and I pleaded again and again to see my brother. Mom began to cry and reached up to grip my right hand. I bent over her, and she leaned my head against her chest, and we wept. I did not notice that I bit my lip until I tasted the blood. My sister sat beside my mother and stayed perfectly still the whole time. Tears streaming down her face were the only sign she was still alive.

The war had claimed its first victim from my family. My kid brother just vanished. The war took him from me, and I was devastated. Even God did not help him. It was His job to protect my little brother, and he had failed. Why? God was not there when my brother needed him. God had not listened to my mother's prayers. She had begged Him to save her son, but God had not answered her. I was angry with God for not listening. I was angry because the Bible promised, "Ask and it shall be given." I was angry with God because he had all the power to cure and heal my brother. And He didn't.

I regret that I did not have the chance to say goodbye to my little brother, but he could not wait for me. He was just a child, but his life was stolen from him. Even as a little boy, Gatdet was smart and strong. I would have liked to meet the man he would have grown to be. I know that he would be stronger than I am. If he were alive today, I know that he could get through anything, no matter what happened.

For months, even a year, his name crept into everyday conversation. I thought about him constantly. Sometimes I would daydream that he just had someplace to go and would be back soon. These delusions brought little comfort. I knew Gatdet was not coming back.

In 1988, six years after the SPLA had shot down the helicopter over our village, the SPLA had swelled to tens of thousands of heavily armed soldiers. Now it returned to attack Nasir once again. Finally, the SPLA defeated the Arab armies in Kuanylualthuan in a year-long battle, one of the bloodiest of the civil wars that claimed thousands of lives.

Even this victory could not change the fact that we had lost absolutely everything. Our livestock was gone, and rain was scarce. Famine began waging its own war. Because of the drought, many people escaped to refugee camps in neighboring countries, but my family decided not to leave. We hoped things would get better and life would return to normal.

Soon food became hard to find. On more than one occasion, my mother gave her family food and left none for herself. Sometimes I pretended that I was full just so she would have something to eat, but my trick never worked. Like most mothers, she knew us inside and out and how much I could eat. She always knew when I was pretending.

To find food, my mother would go with other women to dig out *liews*, a potato-like root that is extremely poisonous if not cooked properly. She would be gone for days collecting *liews* that grow under certain trees in the forest, always on guard for snakes and wild animals. Before the civil war broke out, I never thought I would eat *liews*, but life is strange and unpredictable. I also never thought that my family would lose everything we had, but as the old Nuer saying goes, *"Nguang baoke ka bike wao."* Things come and go.

While Mom searched for *liews*, Dad was trying everything he could to bring food to the table. He tried to hunt using spears, but found that animals were chased away by gunfire. Even lakes and rivers were empty because they were overfished. Soon, the poison plant was our only source of food, and even that became difficult to find. In fact, Dad started to go with Mom when she searched for *liews* to protect her from thieves.

Meanwhile, the SPLA had defeated the Arabs in Kuanylualthuan and took up residence there. With the Arabs gone, life started to return to normal. People began to settle down as those who had once lived in the city began to rebuild their homes. Others returned to their destroyed villages to start again. People once more began to cultivate their farms and plant crops. Our family might rebuild and replant, but I would not be a big brother anymore.

Chapter 4

"Good Morning, Boy Soldier"

In 1989, a couple of months after the Arab armies were defeated in Kuanylualthuan, the SPLA began to recruit again. The war still raged across much of southern Sudan, but this time the SPLA was much more aggressive and went straight to the chief of each village to request a certain number of men for recruits.

Duol, Tut, and Ngut had gone to Itang Refugee Camp in Ethiopia in 1987. When my brother Tut came to visit, my dad, mom, and sister Nyadiew still lived in my Aunt Nyamol's village Lualayiak. I remember that it was the rainy season and we were eating sweet corn. Tut and I had gone to visit Deng, my step-cousin, at his uncle's compound. Shortly after we arrived, I decided to return to our compound on my own. As I approached, my cousin Nyanchar ran toward me, shrieking my name.

"Luk! Lukmaan! Where is Tut?"

"At Deng's compound when I left ..." Before I could finish speaking, she began to drag me back there.

"Come on! Faster!" Her panicked cry scared me.

"Nyanchar, what's wrong? Tell me!"

"No time to talk!" she gasped. "We have to find him before they do!"

"Before who finds him?" Already I had forgotten about the SPLA catching boys to force them to join the army. I may not have known who was after Tut, but I could tell that I was not going to like what I was about to learn. I had never seen Nyanchar so upset.

When we reached Deng's uncle's compound, we found Tut exactly where I had left him in the barn, chatting with Deng. Nyanchar urged

Tut, "Hide! Hide in the woods right away! The chief from our old village is here with a soldier looking for you, Tut. Don't come out of the woods 'til they've gone!" We watched Tut disappear into the dark woods before we took our eyes off him.

Breathing less heavily, she and I walked back toward our compounds, and she began to explain what had frightened her. "I was collecting sweet corn when I saw the chief and a man in a green uniform talking to my parents. The man in the uniform was not a policeman, but he carried a gun. I knew he was a soldier. When I heard the chief ask about Tut, I immediately feared the worst. The army had come to catch 'recruits' and was looking for your brother. I dropped the corn and ran to find you." By the time we reached home, both men had left. Everyone wanted to know where Tut was hiding. Nyanchar explained all that she had seen and that Tut was safe in the bushes.

Later, I learned that my parents had lied to the chief that day. They had told him that Tut had left the previous day to return to the camp in Ethiopia. To protect Tut and keep the chief from discovering my parents' lie, my sister ran to tell the rest of our family, about thirty aunts, uncles, and cousins, what to say if the chief asked about Tut. Unfortunately, the chief did not believe them. He knew families would do anything to protect their kids.

As the soldier had searched from hut to hut, the chief insisted that Tut was still in the compound and began to threaten my parents. "If you won't tell us where he is, we will take three of your cows."

My dad stuck to his story and continued to exchange words with the chief. Eventually, the chief seemed to believe him, though he still had some doubts. The chief then told my father that if Tut were not at the compound when he and the soldier returned in three days, he would fine my father three cows.

An hour later, Tut was back at Deng's uncle's compound, but he did not come home until Deng's cousin made sure the chief had gone. My parents and Tut worked out a plan for his return to camp in Ethiopia. Tut would leave early in the morning, a full day before the chief said he would be back. Just to be safe, they decided that Tut should stay with Deng that night. Even though my parents had known the chief of our old village for a very long time, they did not trust him and knew that he could return at any time.

As expected, the chief came back early, but Tut was safely on his way. The chief announced, "By now, I'm sure that you have told Tut that we are looking for him."

"I told you before, "said my father. "Tut is no longer here."

"Old man," said the solider politely to my dad, "you tell us where your son is."

"My son," Dad replied just as politely, "I told you Tut had gone back to the camp in Ethiopia."

The soldier pressed on. "When we were here before, people told us Tut was here."

My father became angry that the young soldier continued to challenge him so disrespectfully and lost his cool. He shouted, "Then let those people tell you where he is!"

Now the chief spoke. *"Guanduol."* This title of utmost respect recognized my father as being a first-born son, his birthright. "Is it true that your son has gone back to camp?"

"Yes, Chief. He went back to Ethiopia, as I told you."

"Well, we are here to bring Tut to Kuanylualthuan. This letter explains everything," said the chief as he reached into his front pocket. "It is from a general of the SPLA with clear instructions to bring Tut back to Kuanylualthuan. If I am unable to bring him your son, you will be fined three cows. If what you say is true and Tut has returned to camp, then I must take three cows to pay the fine."

"We have no cows for you to take. Not even a barn or a goat. We lost everything in the war."

The chief considered this for a moment and then made his decision. "In that case, you must come to Kuanylualthuan in two days to explain this to the general. Make certain you show up," warned the chief. Then he and the young soldier left.

Two days later, Dad walked more than ten miles to Kuanylualthuan to meet the general and planned to return home the next day. Yet, two days after this meeting, my father still had not returned. On the third day, the chief returned with the soldier but without my dad.

They arrived without warning while my mother was starting a cooking fire for lunch and my sister and I were playing *yiet,* a strategy game with small stones or dried mud playing pieces called cows.

"*Manduol,* Duol's mother. We are here to bring Gatluk with us to Kuanylualthuan. The general wants to see him."

"Why does the general want to see Gatluk if his father is already in Kuanylualthuan?"

"I am only doing what I am told, to bring Gatluk with me. It is getting late. We must go now."

"I still do not understand? Why must you take Gatluk? I haven't finished preparing the food ..." Mom sounded very sad, unsure of herself. "I will make it quick." I could tell Mom was trying to stall the chief so I could at least have food in my belly.

"Nightfall will catch us before we reach Kuanylualthuan as it is. He will eat when we get there."

By now, my sister and I had stopped playing to listen to Mom and the chief talking. This time they had come, not for Tut, but for me. They realized Tut was long gone. They would not keep my dad because he was too old to be recruited into the army. They had come for *me.*

I thought of running and tried to stand, but I felt like I was tied down and could not move. Maybe I was paralyzed by fear. Confused and unable to think, I just sat there with my pebbles, as trapped and defenseless as a baby bird.

Helpless and weeping, my mother held my sister as the two men, twice my size, grabbed me and pulled me away. I was only nine and a half years old.

Just before nightfall, we reached Kuanylualthuan. The soldier took me to a brick building pocked with bullet holes, about fifteen by ten feet, where the other boys were held. The unit's leader, an older Nuer boy named Tang, would have received his manhood marks the following season if he had not been taken by the SPLA. The soldier told Tang my name and that I would sleep there until I was needed in the morning. Tang nodded, and the soldier left.

"Gatluk, you come with me." I followed Tang through the dark into one of the buildings, and he showed me the room I would share with twenty-seven other boys. "This is where you will sleep tonight." My empty stomach started to ache. This was the first time I would sleep in a house made of bricks. It felt like a cave compared with my family home made of mud with a roof of wood and long grass. I did not see my father or the general that night.

Early in the morning, we were jolted awake by a piercing whistle and pounding on the door that sounded like someone trying to kick it down. The other boys rushed to the door, trampling me on the floor. Like wildebeests crossing the Nile, everyone raced and slammed me back on the floor. As a result, I was the very last boy out of the building. Now I learned why everyone was in such a hurry. The last boy was considered late and punished with five lashes across the buttocks. Because this was my first time, I got my first and only warning. Being late a second time would mean five lashes; a third time would be ten, and so on.

We lined up and were led to the field. Not knowing what to do, I just followed the other boys. As the sun rose, we were told to sit. Three men in army uniforms approached us. The bodyguards on either side of the captain carried AK-47s.

"*Sabakaar Jesh-ameer*—good morning, child soldier," the captain began, using an unfamiliar Arabic term. His bossy voice told me disobedience would not be tolerated.

"Good morning, captain," replied all the boys, except me. I remained silent because I did not know what he had said. Then he began to speak to us in Nuer, our native language.

"You are here because we need you. You are here because you will become soldiers and fight Arab ..."

I cannot remember what he said after I was told I was to become a soldier. My mind raced. *What can he mean, "become soldiers"? How can a boy be a soldier? In our culture, nine-year-old boys do not go to war. I have not yet received my manhood marks, so how could I become a soldier? Dad, where are you?* I felt confused and frightened but dared not show this.

After the captain finished, we had midday meal. The food was terrible, just a watery soup of cow meat, coarsely ground husks and hulls, and no salt, not anything like my mother's cooking.

The soldier from yesterday brought me to the general and my father. Maybe now I could go home! At the general's place, I saw many men in uniform sitting under the tree with my dad. The soldier stopped me. I counted as he took five steps toward the general, stomped his foot, and saluted before introducing me as my father's son.

The general eyed me. "He is a big boy." I had always been tall for my age. "We will keep him." He turned to my father. "Old man, your son will stay. You can go home now."

"But my son is very young. He is not even a man yet. What are you going to do with him? He cannot fight. He is still a boy!"

"Things have changed, old man. Boys do not have to be men to fight."

"Take me, then," pleaded my father. "Let my son go home."

"You are too old to be a soldier. You go on home."

Nothing my father could say was going to change the situation. Just like the captain told us on the field that morning, I was about to become a child soldier. Just like that, I was on my own.

I wanted to cry when my father left, but I held my tears. I was determined to show no weakness, but I cried on the inside. Then I panicked. I could not go home with my father! I struggled to wave goodbye. One soldier dragged me by the wrist while another pushed my dad away. Every time I twisted myself away to go hug my dad, the soldier jerked me back. I knew he was about to beat me in front of Dad. All I wanted was to hug my father, but the soldier made a big deal of it. I never did hug Dad goodbye.

Tang greeted me when the soldiers returned me to what had become my unit. I did not want to talk. My lips and tongue felt heavy from sadness. Homesickness began to weaken me. I just wanted to go home, but I could not. Tang explained that lots of boys had these feelings but got over them once they realized there was nothing they could do. I was not sure that I would ever "get over it" anytime soon. I thought about my dad, who would be home soon, and wondered how my mother would react when he arrived without me. Already I missed being a farmer's child. Now, I was a boy soldier.

Chapter 5

The Army Owns Me Now

The next three weeks in Kuanylualthuan introduced me to the army and boot camp. We boy soldiers were told what to do and what not to do. We were told when to eat and even when to use the toilet. (Toilets themselves were foreign to me. Our village did not have plumbing, so we just used the bushes.) We were told when to sleep but found it hard on the cement, where one boy's legs were the next boy's pillow because so many of us were crammed into the room. Despite so many bodies, we were cold without blankets. In the evening, firewood was left to smolder in the windowless room to get rid of the bugs and mosquitoes. Even after much of the smoke had cleared, the bugs came back. Sleep was hard with their biting, the cold, cramp, and stinging eyes.

Every morning, soldiers escorted fifteen to twenty units to the field where we learned military basics. We marched and jogged around the field. We were taught to stand up tall, look straight ahead, and keep our arms by our sides.

More and more boys arrived during the following week, and nothing in my new life became easier. The food was particularly bad. Without any women or girls, traditional chores had to be assigned differently in the army. Older boys were tasked to cook, and young boys, like me, collected firewood. Men and boys were kept separated.

I was overjoyed when Mom came to visit me, though we were prevented from leaving or going anywhere without a guard. During our visit, the guard watched every movement. My new friends were happy when they tried her delicious couscous. She also brought my father's mosquito net and some bedding. Before she left, she told me that everyone at home said hello and that she would be back the next week. I already missed everyone and wanted so badly to go home with her, but I knew that was not possible.

Four days later, I was the last person out of the building again and was whipped with a stick as thick as a man's finger. This punishment was performed on the field in front of everyone. One of the *"Short,"* a police force of sorts made up of older boys, called me forward and told me to lie on my stomach. After he whipped me, I was sent back to the line. I shook with pain but was determined not to cry. I knew that if I cried, they would beat me until I stopped.

During my second week as a soldier, new boys came, and the room our unit shared now housed thirty-two boys. We were packed in like pigs. Sometimes I slept all night just sitting against the wall because there was not enough room on the floor. The worst part was not being allowed to leave the room at night because the door was locked from the outside. Some of the boys could not make it through the night and had to urinate in the room. When that happened, we were all punished and made to stand in the field for an hour with our hands in the air. If we let our hands drop, we would be beaten.

As promised, Mom came back for a second visit. Tang called me over to the visitor's place. I tried to sit still but could not because my bottom still burned from the whipping. This did not escape my mother's notice.

"Magog," she said, using her pet name for me. "What is wrong? Why aren't you sitting still?"

I tried to convince her it was nothing and changed the subject by asking what food she had brought. Couscous! My favorite. Once again, I shared with Tang and my friends.

Mom was still concerned about my butt, but I did not want to tell her what had happened. I did not want her to worry. We talked for a few hours. Before she left, she said that might not be able to come the next week, but my sister would come instead.

The beginning of my third week in Kuanylualthuan was like the others, with new boys arriving every day, but by midweek, people stopped coming. When visitors' day came on Saturday, I expected to see with my mother or my sister. Instead, the captain spoke to us on the field.

"Good morning, soldiers. Today, you will all see the general. He wants to talk to you. Before you see him, you must return to your building, pack your clothes, and stay with your unit. Come back to the field as a unit when you hear the whistle. Do not be late."

All of the units rushed back to their buildings, not entirely sure what was happening. Why would we need our clothes to see the general? Soon, the whistle blew. Tang screamed at us to move faster, so we would not be late. We grabbed our clothes and raced to the field.

The captain acknowledged that all units were on time and then led us to the general in two long lines, one for the boys and one for the men. When we got there, we were ordered to sit. The general strode toward us surrounded by five bodyguards.

"My name is General Koang Chuol. You are here today because you are the future of our country. You are here today because we have a war and an enemy to fight. Our enemies are Arabs who kill our people every day. We fought them here in Kuanylualthuan, and we defeated them. You will be taken someplace to train. When your training is complete, you will receive a weapon and fight the Arabs."

While we were listening to the general, many women and girls began to arrive with food for visitors' day: cornmeal with milk, fish, and sweet corn. Someone must have told them where the general was speaking. He was not pleased by the interruption and told soldiers to make the women and girls leave. Many refused to go without seeing their boys. The soldiers didn't care that they were women and crying, so they beat, slapped and kicked those who refused to leave, even mothers with babies on their backs. Only those who could run away escaped being beaten with sticks. I tried to find my mother in the crowd, but there were too many people. Then we were ordered not to look back at them.

"You are leaving today," the general continued. "You will join other cadets when you arrive at your destination. I wish you all good luck on your journey." He did not tell us where we were going.

Apparently, we were to leave immediately. Units dissolved, and new units of thirty-two were formed from a random and scary mix of men and boys. Some already knew each other. Most were much bigger than we were. After the rosters were written, we were ordered to line up. Then, unit after unit, we began our journey, we little boys pushing our short legs to keep up with the men. We did not know what to expect next.

The first day, we did not go far and settled in a nearby village before the sun set. Unit leaders called our names both at bedtime and each morning to be sure everyone had stayed with his unit. The next morning, we were awakened earlier than usual. It was still dark, but we packed our mosquito nets and headed for the road. We walked ten hours a day without a break for lunch. This continued nearly every day for almost two weeks. After the first week on the road eating only one meal a day, some of us younger boys were too weak to push any further. We had to take a day off every two days that we walked. That helped, but only a little.

By now, my ankles had swollen so badly from days of walking that I hurt too much to carry my blanket and mosquito net. One of the men in my unit, Jal, nicknamed Jalbhar because he was so tall, knew my mother and father. He became not only a friend but like a brother to me, the only person who looked after me on the way from southern Sudan to Ethiopia. He helped me to carry my things and made sure I walked ahead of him on the road. Jal pushed me to keep going when no one else did. If it were not for him, I could easily have been left in the middle of nowhere. Jal helped me to feel safe, and I adored him.

When I asked him where we were going, he said it felt as though the road were leading to Ethiopia. He went on to tell me about his sister who lived in a camp there. When he visited her, he always used the road that followed the Sobat River. He had heard that people used the road we were on when the river flooded. If it turned out that we were heading to Ethiopia, Jal was sure he could find a way to tell his sister and my brothers to come visit us. The thought of seeing my brothers in the Itang Refugee Camp felt good, but the good feeling did not last long. Soon the endless hunger and walking wiped it from my mind.

We came to the Laaw River, a small river that flowed into the Sobat River, but it was too deep and flowed too fast to be crossed safely. During our attempts to cross it, one boy washed away. A man tried to grab him, but the water raged and pulled the boy under. It was discouraging to lose one of our own before facing the Arabs. Something had to be done to cross the hungry canal so we would not lose anyone else. We went to work collecting rushes and other long grasses along the edge of the canal to build boats to float us. The rest of us crossed safely on the two five-man rafts we made.

Weather did not stop us. We kept going no matter how hard it rained.

Our baggage—a blanket, a bed sheet, and a mosquito net—soaked through and became heavier. We carried no water, no weapon, and no uniform. Barefoot, I still wore the same shorts and T-shirt from the day of my capture nearly a month earlier. The worst was sleeping with a wet blanket and mosquito net at night. By evening when we reached our destination, the sun had already set and we had no way to dry anything. When it rained at night, there was nowhere to go. We would stay in our mosquito net and try to squeeze out as much water as we could before we headed out in the morning.

One night while we slept, it started to pour. Strong winds pounded our mosquito nets and, even with help from the boy I shared with, we could not hold on to it. We heard other people struggling to hold down their nets, too, but the wind was too strong. Then we heard footsteps of people who could not take any more wind and rain running to the barn filled with cows and goats. We followed them and slept with the goats that night. Even though the goats stepped on us and urinated everywhere, we were warmer than in the bitter wind and rain outside.

Farther down the road, we found fields of corn. Because we were always hungry, we grabbed ears as we walked by. At first, I didn't feel too bad, but then I realized that I was stealing—and more and more often. One time, we came through a cornfield, and the owner was in it. When the first units had filled their hands, the owner tried to protect his corn. He yelled and cursed and swung his machete to chase us out, but he was outnumbered. Every time he chased some of us away, more of us snatched corn. We robbed him in the middle of the day. I felt sorry for the man who could not protect his corn from the hungry army of ants who stole from him. And I was one of them. I had changed. Right and wrong that I had known so well had changed. I could not escape this. The army owned me, both body and mind.

Chapter 6

I Am Trained to Hate

A week and a half after leaving Kuanylualthuan, we still had no idea how far we were going. I only knew I was a long way from home. I wondered whether my mother had come for visitors' day. If she had, she was surely chased off by soldiers. I hoped they had not beaten her.

A few days later, we settled in a village for the night where the captain told the unit leaders we would stay for two days. We would not have to walk! What we did not know was that we were in the last village before the Ethiopian border. We were given two days' rest only because we now faced a fourteen-hour walk.

That morning, we lined up as usual and headed down the road, but now as we walked, we saw no villages. Instead, we went deeper and deeper into the forest surrounded by long grasses and unfamiliar trees so big they blocked the sun. Everything was strangely quiet. All we heard were our footsteps and birdsong. The birds were different colors from the ones I was used to and had different voices.

We walked steadily toward our destination, where other cadets were already living. It was now past noon, and the last thing we wanted was for night to fall while we were still on the road. If it got dark before we reached the training camp, the bears, hyenas, and wild dogs would be happy to fill their bellies with our flesh.

When we were close enough, we walked the man-made road that led straight to the camp. Nearby, we saw men and boys climbing out of the forest carrying firewood for cooking. Many of them were from Nuba, Dinka, Nuer, and other tribes. More and more cadets gathered around us as we made our way into camp. Some just shouted or threw their hands in the air shouting, "SPLM!" I guess they were just excited to see us. We were directed to the field with all the other units and, even after waking fourteen hours, had to stay standing until all the other units arrived.

Once everyone was in place, our captain told us we had made it to training camp. He then reported us to the captain in control of the camp. After he welcomed us, the camp captain told each of our units to follow the men who would show us where we would spend the night. The sun was setting, so we made our mosquito nets ready. After a grueling two weeks on the road with bare feet dry, calloused, and cut by grass, I just wanted to sleep as long as I could.

The next morning, we were sent to the field. As newcomers, we stood apart from the others. The camp captain told us to divide ourselves into groups of men and boys, depending on whether we had our manhood marks. I had none. In this camp, men and boys did not live together. The soldiers who had been leaders of our units left with the captain who brought us. This was the last time I saw them. I am not sure if they went back to Kuanylualthuan or were sent somewhere else.

We boys were incorporated into the existing boys' units. The men were also placed into existing units. Boys in my unit were all from different tribes. The unit leader was from Nuba. Six other boys were Nuer like me. Only one was from my village. It was hard to make friends with other boys from different tribes because I did not speak their languages.

After three days at the training camp, I felt I was settling into my new unit. Like the other units, we had just one house, about ten feet by fifteen feet. When it rained, we packed ourselves indoors; otherwise, we slept outside. Our cooking area had a roof but no walls. We cooked our food in a cut-off barrel and then ate off brown sacks on the ground. Bean soup with oil and salt was served in a big ammunition container the military used for carrying bullets.

The Itang Refugee Camp in Ethiopia was just eight to ten miles from the training camp. I did not see Jal much after we arrived, but I wondered if he had found anyone who could tell his sister or my brothers that we had been caught and brought to the training camp.

New cadets continued to arrive every week. Training did not begin until the fourth week. Every morning at five o'clock, we were awakened by two whistle blasts about five minutes apart. We had to be ready before the second whistle blew. Anyone still sleeping after the second whistle would be beaten by boys appointed as police. These boys were crazy. They would beat stragglers without mercy and seemed to enjoy every moment. Anyone who stayed asleep would be beaten, no questions asked.

Training in the morning always started with jogging and marching around the field while singing military songs. Many of those we learned were about killing Arabs. They were littered with curses and insulting names for Arabs. Once the jogging and marching drills were finished, the captain gave the morning speech. I do not remember much from these speeches, but I will never forget being told this: "Kill or be killed!"

Once in the field, we were expected to be silent. Questions were not tolerated. Each unit had two trainers who held absolute authority over our every action. We called them *Taleamgy*, Arabic for *trainer*. They seemed to be disciples of the "Shoot first—ask questions later" mentality. For any infraction, we were beaten first and spoken to later.

Once while standing in line, I reached down to swat at the flies feeding on the small open wound on my leg. People surrounded me, so I did not notice one of the trainers walking through the lines. When I stood back up, he was standing over me. I will never forget the terrifying madness in his eyes. His eyes bulged out of his head before he beat me like a dog.

"Fly must eat because we eat," was his only explanation.

No matter what our task—pushups, sit-ups, running, climbing mountains—anything—we were beaten if we did not perform exactly right. Even right after lunch, we were forced to keep drilling. I hated being made to jump like a frog then because it made us throw up.

We trained every day until midday, when we were given an hour break for lunch. At night, the whistle was blown twice, first as a warning to those who fell asleep and then again one minute later to assemble on the field. The police beat anyone they found sleeping. If a name was called and the boy was not there, he would be beaten, even if he was unlucky enough to be relieving himself in the bushes before the whistle was blown. There was no acceptable excuse for any situation. We were beaten again and again for months until we got used to it.

When I saw Jal six weeks after we had separated, he still had not found anyone to deliver a message to our families. I thought a lot about my family back home during those rare times I was alone. Like many kids, I missed them terribly. Sometimes I wished they were close enough to visit me like in Kuanylualthuan. Mostly, though, I thought about why I was there. I cried and cried even though I was showing weakness—but I made very sure no one saw me cry. I found some privacy under the mosquito net, by going to the bathroom in the bushes, and by pulling a blanket over my head to make sure no one heard my sobs. Other boys may have heard. We all went through it. If security caught us, they would drag us out into the field and beat us.

What benefit would I get from being angry at the police? If I showed anger, I'd be in more trouble for disrespect. I had to control my emotions to avoid more beatings. I had to control my emotions to survive.

As the training intensified, the beatings became nothing. Every time I was beaten, I just became more resistant to the pain. All of us got used to it. This method of teaching made it easy to be angry at the Arabs we cursed and sang about killing. The songs we sang stuck in my head. In my village, a boy was just a boy until he reached manhood. Here we were taught, "A boy with a gun is a man who will be feared." Guns were everything. A man without a gun was nothing. I could not wait to get my own AK-47, which would mean I could fight like a man. Of course, it weighed about twenty pounds, and I weighed only a hundred, but didn't think about that. Once I was issued my gun, I would be able to do all the things I thought about and talked about. I would fight and kill Arabs. These thoughts never would have crossed my mind if I were still at home in my village surrounded by people who cared for me.

Now the captain's words started to make sense: "Kill or be killed!" *I have to kill Arabs before they kill me.* And if I had to die, I would die fighting. This hatred was a side of myself I had never known before being taken to the training camp. Sometimes I scared myself thinking such ugly thoughts with my nine-year-old mind. Yet when we were on the field, we were treated like men and had to act accordingly. "Be a man. Ignore the pain."

Was I just a boy pretending to be a man, or had I become a half-man? I was now nearly ten years old, not yet a man, but I was treated like a man on the field. I was being forced to act like a man. I was so confused. I did not know how to think of myself, nor did I know anything about brainwashing. I only knew that the hatred kept me strong and kept me going. Little by little, day by day, revenge grew inside me like a fire. After a while, I even stopped thinking about going home.

We were taught to fight, but not indiscriminately. "Our enemies are Arabs," our officers warned. "Not our brothers." Fighting within camp was dealt with like anything else. Fighters were beaten and told never to fight a brother. We never doubted that our true enemies were the Arabs.

I did not notice my own hatred growing. The Arabs had done horrible things to my people. Every time they were mentioned, I thought of the brother they stole from me. They killed my kid brother, and now I wanted revenge. I wanted to kill the Arabs who took Gatdet. I had learned to hate, just like the enemy.

Chapter 7

Saved by Sickness

I had been at the training camp five months before word that I was nearby reached my brothers Duol, Tut, and Ngut in the Itang Refugee Camp in Ethiopia. Unaware that I had been "recruited" to the army, they reacted with shock and disbelief to news of my capture. When Jal's sister visited a few weeks later, she brought some nylon shorts and cotton t-shirts my brothers had given her for me. I learned that my brothers could not safely visit me for fear that they, too, would be conscripted. Even though I was only eight or ten miles from them, I could not leave the training camp. It would take a miracle to see my brothers. At least news would reach my parents that I had been brought to the army training camp in Ethiopia, that I was still alive.

About a month after Jal's sister visited me, I fell sick, wracked by diarrhea, fever, weakness, loss of appetite, and a painfully stiff spine. We had nearly finished training, but I could not bend my back or move my neck. Jal became sick, too, about a week after I did. Since we had no clinic, everyone who was sick was just brought to an awful grass-covered hut away from the camp. We lay on the earth floor on leftover feed sacks with no mosquito net to protect us. The forty or so sick people, including those who could not feed themselves or make it to the toilet, were left to fend for themselves. No one helped us or cared about us. The captain came by to check only after he was told that four men and seven boys had died. We learned this when the morning crew came to deliver food and remove the bodies.

The captain ordered us to be carried to the hospital in the refugee camp. Jal was strong enough to walk, but four men were going to have to carry me with a blanket. Before they came, something amazing happened.

An old man dressed in black pants and a long-sleeved, white shirt watched me struggling to get up. When he saw that my back and neck had seized, he called out, "Son of my brother, you sit still." He walked behind me, pressed his knee into the middle of my back, and pulled my shoulders back with both hands. My back began to loosen from the intense pressure of his knee. My body felt like it had been shocked by electricity. As soon as he let go of me, I felt relief. He held my arm as I stood up because I was so skinny and lightheaded. Someone gave me a stick to steady my trembling legs, but I do not know who it was. The old man had disappeared, but I was still standing. He must have been an angel sent to free me from this fate. He gave me a window to fly free of pain.

One of the men with the blanket came just as we were ready to leave. "We are here to carry you. Lie down."

Without hesitating, I said, "I can walk." Even Jal tried to convince me to let them carry me. I didn't budge. Finally, they decided they would walk behind me and carry me if I got tired.

It was a long, long eight-to-ten-mile walk to the refugee camp after being sick on the ground. I wore only a sheet wrapped around me, but at least I did not have to be carried. We took a break after each mile and did not arrive until midday, when the doctors were on break. In Africa, people work until noon and have a break until 2:00 p.m. We sat in the waiting room and had milk for lunch.

Once the doctors returned, each of us was given a card with our name, and then we waited our turn. This was the first time I had been to a doctor since my birth. When it was my turn, I was called to sit in a chair, and a doctor in a long, white coat examined me. He gave me a piece of paper and told me to bring it to a room on the left end of the building.

Leaning on my stick, I slowly made my way to the pharmacy, a room full of small bottles handled by a woman and man in white jackets. He took my paper, and then I sat until my name was called. Jal waited for medication, too.

Those who had been carried had to stay in the hospital until their conditions improved. Those of us who had walked were taken to one of the army's compounds after receiving our medicine. I was so glad Jal was with me. Not only was he the only person I knew, but he knew where my brothers lived. Meanwhile, my brothers and Jal's sister had no idea we were just a few blocks away.

An official asked if any of us had relatives at the camp. Jal raised his hand, along with a few others, but I stayed quiet, hoping Jal would speak for me. When the soldier told Jal to wait while someone was found to escort him to his sister's compound (so the army would know his whereabouts), I worried that I would be separated from my friend. I shouldn't have worried. Jal spoke up and explained that he knew where my brothers were.

After more waiting, the soldier returned and told us he could not find an escort. The other soldiers were busy or bathing in the river. The soldier decided that he himself would take us and grabbed our things.

When we arrived at Jal's compound soon after, Jal called out to the huts in front of us. A woman came out of one of the huts and ran to hug Jal. She was tall, but not as tall as Jal.

"Who is this?" she asked.

"This is Duol's brother," said Jal. Now the light rain began to pour like water out of a jar. The soldier confirmed that Jal would be staying here; then he left. We waited for the rain to let up before Jal's sister, Nyakong, took me to my brothers.

As we left, Jal reminded me to take my medicines every day. I followed her a couple of blocks to my brothers' compound.

"Hello, Chol! Are you home?" Nyakong called as the rain again began to pound. Chol opened the door to let her in but did not recognize me at all. I had not seen my aunt in many years, so I was not surprised at her reaction. I looked nothing like the Gatluk she had known; now I was taller, skinny, and sickly. I was too cold to say anything. The sheet I wore now dripped water, and my teeth chattered.

"Chol, this is Gatluk!"

My aunt ran to hug me, screaming at the top of her lungs, "Oh, my sister's son! Oh, my sister's son! I did not recognize you. I did not know it was *Lukmaan* (woman judge)." She spat on my head in Nuer greeting and continued to scold herself for not recognizing me, tears rolling down her cheeks. Despite my sickness, my spirit felt joy knowing I was again with my family. I had feared we'd never see each other again.

Ngut was the first of my three brothers to come to Chol's hut. He hugged me and kept looking at me. By now, I shivered uncontrollably, so Chol made tea to warm me and put it on the floor in front of me. I reached for the small metal cup and brought it halfway to my lips before it jiggled loose from my shivering hands. Tea spilled everywhere. My first cup of tea would have to wait.

My brothers took me to their hut and replaced my wet sheet with a warm, dry blanket. All three sat across the room and gazed at me. Tut said, "If I had known the army was going to take you, I would not have left." I did not respond because I did not know what to say. Duol and Ngut, whom I had not seen for a couple of years, sat in silence. Our happiness filled the room with no need for words. The reunion would have been perfect if my parents and sister had been there, too. For now, being reunited with my brothers and not feeling alone for the first time in months was pure relief.

Still cold and shivering under the blanket, but fed with my aunt's food, I told my brothers I wanted to sleep. I took my medicine and closed my eyes, safe at last.

In the morning, I took my medicine and tried to eat the cornmeal mush like a smoothie that Aunt Chol had made. It was too sweet. I was not used to sweet foods. Plus, we never had breakfast at the village or training camp, and my appetite was gone from being sick.

After two weeks in the refugee camp, I showed no improvement. I worried that I was too sick for the medicine to work. The card I had received at the hospital instructed me to return in three weeks to pick up my medicines. Duol made the trip to get them for me. After five weeks, I started to feel a bit better, but still I had not seen Jal. I wondered if the soldier had ever gone back to get him.

A few weeks later, Duol ran into Jal's sister and learned that Jal had been taken back to the training camp after he recovered. I feared that the soldiers would come and look for me now that I was beginning to feel better. Fortunately, Jal had never shown them my brothers' compound. The soldiers had no way to find me. Jal had saved me, but I never saw him again.

After Jal was taken back, the cadets at the camp finished training and were shipped to the next training camp, where they would receive their guns. From there, they would be sent to southern Sudan to fight Arabs.

But I had been left behind. I had lost my chance to avenge my brother and fight for my people.

At the same time, I had made it out of the army after seven and a half months. I am sure that I would have been killed if I had stayed. Being only ten years old, how could I have protected myself? What could I have done as well as or better than a grown man? The army needed anyone who could shoot. They didn't care that their soldiers were children.

Little by little, I regained my strength and put on some weight, but physically, I was not yet ready to walk many miles across the border back to southern Sudan and my parents. During the day, I would go to the bakery where my Uncle Gach worked. He is my uncle, but we are the same age. Mostly, I just sat around unless they needed a hand. I knew I had to find something to do to take my mind off the ugly and scary memories in my head.

Gach's workplace was close to the flea market where people sold all kinds of things: foods, soaps, salt, and so forth. When I tired of sitting, I walked around the market looking at the interesting things for sale. I was curious about selling salts, but I did not have money to start.

My uncle agreed to loan me five *birr,* about five cents, to buy salts when he was paid at the end of the month. I was excited to be able to buy my ingredients: three cups of salt, hot peppers for flavor, and a bag to store everything. For half a birr, I rented a wood grinder to mix peppers into the salt. To make it look fresh, I added some water. At the market, salt vendors lined either side of the path, facing each other. I found an empty place between two other boys. Even though most of the customers were women who did the cooking, only a few men and boys sold salts.

Selling was all about body language. The most common selling technique was to call attention to yourself and your wares by yelling to the passing customers, "My salt will give women babies!" I quickly realized that if I were going to make any money, I would have to learn this technique. Within a week, I was able to pay back the money I had borrowed from my uncle. On a good day, I could earn between twelve and seventeen birr. It was not difficult to convince my uncle to try selling salts, since he was earning only one birr a day at the bakery. However, he was not very good at it, so he went back to his other job.

One day, while I was selling salts as usual, my cousin Nyaiany, Chuol's daughter, found me at the market to tell me that my mother had come to the refugee camp. At first, I did not believe her and stayed focused on my customers. She told me that my parents had learned of my reunion with my brothers from people traveling back and forth to southern Sudan. For the first time in her life, my mother had made the journey to Ethiopia—a two-week trek if walking fast—to see my brothers and me. Now she waited for me in the compound. I still did not completely believe my cousin, but I gathered my salts and rushed back to find the mother I hadn't seen for almost a year.

When I spied Mom, I dropped my salts and threw myself at her to hug her. She spat on my head. The rest of our joy I cannot describe. She assured me that my dad and sister were fine. She said my aunt Nyamol. Dad's oldest sister, who was like a grandmother to me, was also well and missed me.

Even with Mom around, I kept selling salts during the day to keep my mind off everything I had gone through in the army. A couple of months later, after I had been in the camp for about six months, Mom decided it was time to return home to southern Sudan. It was now 1990. We bought some clothes and headed back to the border crossing. It was not safe to return to my aunt's village, Lualayiak, so Mom brought Tut and me to my Uncle Gony's village, Muon. A few months later, Tut would have to return to the refugee camp, a safe haven from the SPLA because the United Nations would not allow recruitment from the camp.

My father, mother, sister and I moved to Muon, less than a two-day walk away. I had grown a lot in the year I had been separated from my family and was no longer the little boy who was dragged away from his home. Though I had completely recovered from my physical illness, my bad memories of being a soldier always shadowed me like a hyena in the forest. I did not show these emotions to my family.

Chapter 8

Caught Between Famine and War

A few months after we moved to my uncle's village, we learned that Tut had been abducted from the Ethiopian refugee camp by the Red Shoulder, a branch of the SPLA formed to kidnap boys and men. He had been taken to the Bonga's training camp, a different camp from the one where I had been held. We had believed that the refugee camp was a safe place for my brother, but in reality, the SPLA had the means to abduct people anywhere. When hunger started forcing more people to the refugee camp months later, my parents hesitated to go. Food kept getting harder to come by. Eventually, we had no choice but to return to Ethiopia, a week's walk away.

Once back at the refugee camp, I again sold salts and started selling oil, too. Mom made her famous black liquor to sell. Our living conditions had improved, for we now had food, safety, and a little money. After nearly seven months, however, we still had no word from Tut. The Bonga's training camp was hidden deep within the forest. Only those people who had been shown it could find it. Also, the army made it very difficult for anybody to leave the camp. People who might try to escape would have to walk at night through the forest without a trail or directions. Escapees spotted by soldiers would be shot on sight—if they managed to avoid being mauled and eaten by hyenas, bears, and lions.

Then one day, I had just returned from bathing in the Baro River with my dad and sat in the shade of a dry grass fence. My mom and cousin Nyayiony sat in front Aunty Chol's hut as she cooked dinner. Our fence gate creaked open. Tut! He had escaped! I could not believe my eyes. It was really him! I ran to hug him. Nyayiony and Nyadiew ran behind me, hugging him as happy tears washed their faces. I felt their emotion but held my tears. Mom, Dad, and Aunty spat on his head in traditional greeting. As neighbors learned of his arrival, they came to greet him too. We were so surprised and happy to have him home.

But Tut looked drawn and gaunt from lack of sleep and not enough food. His cheekbones stuck out of his face because he had lost so much weight, and his feet bled with oozing sores from walking without shoes. He was covered in bug bites. Within a few days, Tut started to feel sick. His body got hot, and he threw up. We thought it must be an allergy to the bug bites and did not take it very seriously. Even Tut did not think it was a big deal and started to feel better.

When his sickness worsened, he went to the United Nations clinic in the camp. Their medicine seemed to help, at least for a while. For weeks, his condition fluctuated, each time leaving him a little worse. After four and a half months of this condition, Tut was fighting for his life. The hospital could not figure out what was wrong with him, and the medicines the doctor had given him stopped working. Maybe they didn't have the right diagnostic equipment, or maybe they were not educated enough. Mom and Dad could not watch him die. They had to do something.

My parents decided to bring him to Kuanylualthuan, where he would have a chance to be taken to Kenya for treatment. After the Arabs were defeated in 1989, the United Nations had established a medical center capable of transporting seriously ill patients to better-equipped facilities.

My parents collected some money and rented a dugout canoe with my Aunt Nyanguda's help. Because Tut could not walk, it would be easier to bring him to Kuanylualthuan by canoe on the Sobat River, a three-to-five-day trip, instead of being jostled overland during a weeklong walk. Duol and my parents went along to paddle while my sister, my brother Ngut and I waited at the Itang Refugee Camp.

Duol returned with the dugout a couple of weeks later, but even after a month, we heard nothing from my parents. Then after another week, my Aunty Nyanguda came to our compound while we ate dinner. She sat with Aunt Chol and waited for us to finish. "I heard news of Tut from a person who came yesterday from Kuanylualthuan …" She paused.

Silence.

I knew something was wrong. If she were going to tell us Tut was getting better, she would not have waited for us to finish eating. She would not have paused.

"Tut passed away last week," she said. Tears drifted down her cheeks.

For two hours, we sat there silently crying. My heart was torn apart. I could remember so clearly Tut being gently placed in the dugout, then Duol paddling until I could no longer see them on the river. I had not known that was the last time I would see my brother. Now I had lost a second brother, and I never got to say goodbye.

When Mom and Dad returned a month later, we grieved for Tut again. What was left of our family was together, but Tut and Gatdet would always be missing. Three weeks after my parents' return, we had a prayer for the whole family to say a final goodbye, an emotional day for all our relatives and us. Everyone wiped away tears. Tut had been a loveable brother and son. He was soft-spoken and easy-going. I raged at God who let this good brother die. *Why have you created my brothers and taken they from us so early? What have they done?* I could not remember the Bible verse that day, but I do remember the preacher saying, "Tut is in a better place now. We do not have to worry about him anymore."

If Tut was safe, we were not. Before the year was out, we would be dealt another blow—the Ethiopian Revolution of 1991. Civil war had torn Ethiopia for nearly twenty years. Now Chairman Meles Zenawi led the Ethiopian People's Revolutionary Democratic Front (EPRDF) to overthrow the anti-democracy regime. We heard stories of more than a million people killed in Addis Ababa when the city was overrun by tanks and captured between 1974 and 1991, when the war had started. Ethiopia had become dangerous. Even the camps no longer offered a safe, stable place. Anything could happen.

All refugees had to return to South Sudan or travel across the borders to Kenya to escape the warfare. But back in South Sudan, there was nothing to eat because everything was gone or destroyed. The United Nations tried to send food, but it was not enough. The old airport in Kuanylualthuan was not large enough for the main food planes to land, so supplies sent by the United Nations had to be dropped from the air. Now many people died as famine claimed its victims.

After a year in Muon struggling every day just to have enough to eat, my dad was fed up.

"I refuse to die waiting for UN food to come!" he growled. "My father did not raise me with UN food. It is because of the war that we lost everything. God gives this land to men to feed their families. I am going to do what my father taught me—farming. That was how I fed you. You young people talk about school and government. Can you see what those people who went to school to run the government have done to us? They are thieves and killers. In my day, nobody stole things. Things like this would not have happened!"

I had never seen my father so angry before. He raged against all the evil things beyond his control happening around us. He was terrified by how violent the world had become. I cannot blame him for feeling the way he did. Human beings had become like wild animals—eat or be eaten. More than anything, Dad wished things would return to normal. Unfortunately, our lives were far from getting better, and he had to accept that the world was a crazy place. Our only choice was to live through it, one way or another.

Chapter 9

Left for Dead

In 1994, my parents very nearly lost their third son, and my life changed forever. I was thirteen years old.

Rumors had started to spread that the Arab militias were again attacking villages. They would attack and then disappear, traveling only at night to avoid being seen. But we were a two-day walk on foot from where those rumors started, so we were not worried that Arabs would reach us. Plus, we were close to Kuanylualthuan and the SPLA. We thought we were safe. Little did we know that the Arab militias were making their way straight toward our village.

The day of the attack started very strangely. The morning fog was not like any I had ever seen. It was during the dry season and not likely to rain, yet the fog was thick enough to block the sun and turn it red. This was rare during the dry season. The elders began to talk of what it could mean. In Nuer culture, the people depended upon natural signs to know when to plant and when to clear. A red sun was an omen, to be sure, and the elders knew from experience that it was a bad sign that could mean death. As the sun rose, the fog remained instead of burning off. That morning, just like every other morning, we woke up and did our chores as usual. I collected cow dung.

That afternoon, about three o'clock, my cousin Wal and I were fishing with a friend by the river. We spread a net weighing about forty pounds to block the flow of the river, only a hundred and fifty yards across. The fish, about two feet long, piled up. This good catch would feed our families.

Suddenly, machine gun fire roared from every direction. No one knew which way to run. People panicked, slipped on fish, and ran for their lives. Wal and I ran up from the riverbank where we had been fishing. I could see people running. Without thinking, we ran to follow them. People who were shot fell to the right and to the left. Those still alive dragged themselves, leaving a trail of blood. Some men tried to face the militias, but they were outnumbered. It was not long before it was every man for himself.

We raced to the bushes for cover and found my sister, who had been separated from my mom. We could not talk, only pant. I did not even ask where Mom was. I was just glad that my sister was alive. We kept running. My best friend, Puoch, was running alone when he joined us. There were five of us: Puoch and my fishing friend Koang on my right and my sister on my left, with my cousin Wal in front of me. I made sure I could see him. He was only ten years old, the only boy and youngest of all his siblings, so I was like a big brother to him. I was determined that he not be left behind or separated from us. Together we ran as Arabs chased us through the bushes. We dared not catch our breath. Too soon, Arabs were only four hundred yards behind us. I could hear the screams as they shot people still alive.

Suddenly, a searing pain flashed in my hip. I was knocked out cold by the impact of the bullet. My blood boiled hot. *I've been shot.* My body throbbed like all the drums in the world beating at once as the bullet tore through my leg. Then, silence. Everything just stopped. Silence. Guns firing and people screaming just stopped. Nothing seemed to happen around me. Nothing at all. I was unconscious.

I do not remember falling to the ground on my back. I did not know that the bullet had shattered my left hip and lodged in my leg. I had not heard the gun, but I smelled the gunpowder as I became conscious. Now I heard people crying and screaming my name.

"Gatluk! Get up!" screamed, Wal, Puoch, and my sister. I tried to rise, but fell. I tried again, but could not stand up to try to walk. I could no longer feel my leg. Blood soaked my clothes, the ground, and my hands. Wal, Puoch and my sister drew my arms over their skinny shoulders to carry me, but they were too small and exhausted from running to support me.

Now we could hear the Arabs yelling, "Over, over," as they closed in on us. I was slowing down my family.

"Go! Run!" I whispered. Silent tears ran down their faces. They still struggled to carry me.

"Put me down! Go! Run!" I screamed. They didn't move. "If you stay, we all die. If you go, only one of us dies." I knew beyond all doubt that I would die. I will never forget the horrified looks on my sister and friends' faces as they ran. They knew they might never again see me alive.

By now, I knew that my life was out of my hands. So totally helpless and scared, all I could do was just lie in my own blood and wait for the militia to come and finish me off. I heard the militia voices louder and louder as they came closer. Nothing could stop them from killing me now. Strangely, this knowledge made me feel calm. I accepted that I would not escape death, and faced it. My old army training rushed into my head: *"Kill or be killed." The speeches now make sense. I am going to die.*

Before the Arab militias found me, I wanted to pray. I closed my eyes and said the first thing that came to mind. *"Please, Father, forgive them, for they know not what they do."* What! I could not believe that I had just asked God to forgive the people who had killed my brother and shot me. How could this prayer be the one prayer that came to mind? Who asks God to forgive the person who shot him while he is still bleeding in agony? Why did I not ask God to burn these people in hell? And why did I not ask God to save my life? Before I opened my eyes, I had another thought: play dead. I did not consciously decide this. I just know for certain that the prayer and the idea of playing dead were all God's plan.

I had learned how to play dead from a wildcat. We carried spears when we herded our animals in case we needed to spear fish in the river or protect ourselves against any wildcats. One of the cats always played dead when it saw us. We would stab it with spears, but it would not move. When we returned to it later, it was nowhere to be found. Just like that wildcat, I would play dead to stay alive. I had no idea if the trick would work.

Footsteps came toward me. The Arab militias returned and found me lying on my stomach with my head turned toward my right shoulder. I kept my eyes closed and lay very still, barely breathing. One of the soldiers stabbed me in the chest, just under my arm, to see if I were still alive. He started to stab me again when another man said something in Arabic. I later learned that he said, "Let's go. He's dead."

The stab wound was not deep because my rib stopped the knife. I lay still and did not move an inch of my body. If I had, I would not be telling this today. I had thought my life was over, but I was wrong. I was wrong when I said my life was out of my hand because it never was in my hand. My life was and is in the hand of the Man Above.

I was blessed to be born into a devoted Christian family who lived each day committed to the Ten Commandments and the Word of God. My family raised us to be faithful and good Christians. My parents' favorite commandment—and mine—is "Love your neighbor as you love yourself." I carried this commandment in my heart each day everywhere I went. My parents deeply believed that a heart filled with love represented our God who gave His only son to die for our sins. We knew God loves us.

I came to know Christ as my Lord and Savior at the age of three. The church was in front of our compound. My brother Duol was a choir captain. In our compound, missing Sunday services was out of the question. I would come to love going to church so much that I would take off running there whenever I heard someone playing the church drums. I especially loved the choir singing. As I grew, my attachment to God and my faith grew deeper and deeper. After I was baptized, I opened my heart to God and became closer to Him. I knew God was a loving God.

Even now.

The militia left to kill more of my people instead of wasting time with a kid they thought was already dead. Despite the raging pain, I continued to lie still, eyes closed, in case more soldiers came. I dared not move in case they noticed my new position. Besides, with a shattered hip, I knew I could not get very far.

The African sun beat down, drying the blood on my hands while I lay in the dirt, perfectly still and straining to hear. Long after I heard no guns, maybe an hour and a half, I opened my sticky eyes. Maybe the militia would still come back for me. Playing dead had worked so far, but why take chances? I lay still, quietly panting though the pain.

Hours later, I sluggishly raised my head to look around. Nothing. Groggy with pain and dehydration, I pulled myself to sit up. *My cat trick worked. They did not kill me. I am alive! I cannot believe it! I am still alive!*

Now, as night began to fall, so did my real battle to stay alive. The pain in my right hip felt like fiery spears. My tongue stuck to the roof of my mouth, and I could not swallow. No water. No help. I was on my own, surrounded by the bodies of dead people. Who were they? Would any of my family or relatives be among these dead? I wondered whether my family and especially my sister Nyadiew and Cousin Wal had escaped. Later I would learn that my friends Wiyual and Bol, both my age, had been murdered. We used to fish together and sing in the church choir. Other neighbors and friends from the village and church had also been massacred.

First, I needed to move. I would not last the night if I stayed where I was. Ravenous hyenas would come out at dusk, eager to feed on my wounded flesh. I knew that I could survive the night only by crawling to the top of a nearby termite hill, a sandy mound about two meters high. Being off the ground would offer me some protection.

Through the stabbing pain, I dragged myself backward to the nearest termite hill and inched to the top. I grabbed a stick on my way so I could protect myself. Hyenas do not usually hunt humans, but if you are defenseless, they will eat you.

I could not think right because of the pain and hunger and thirst. I was tired and weak from the blood loss, but I knew I must not sleep if I wanted to stay alive. Somehow, I remembered a story of people drinking their urine to stay hydrated when they ran out of water. I drank my urine in my cupped hands. It was warm and salty, but at least it was wet. I had to be careful not to drink too much because I did not know how soon I would be found. I needed the urine to last.

As darkness fell, hyenas trotted on from every direction, laughing to each other. The bright moon shone clearly on the ugly beasts as they plowed through the grass strewn with the many, many dead bodies of men, women, and children. Then I could hear hyenas crunching human bones with their teeth. With all the bodies available to the horrible animals, I hoped they would not waste their energy chasing live prey like me. Yet I could be next at any moment.

Soon they smelled my trail of blood and edged toward me. Their glowing eyes surrounded my termite hill. When they tried to climb up to me, I beat them with my stick. "Go away," I tried to shout with my dried tongue. I beat the stick against the ground, but it did not make much of a thump. The hyenas shrieked and giggled as again and again they approached me. Again and again, I beat them off. I do not know where I found the strength.

Eventually, the hyenas lost interest in me and returned to feast on the dead bodies. Throughout the night, they checked on me to see whether I had died. Each time, they found me still alive and returned to the easy-to-eat corpses.

That was the longest night of my life. Every tiny movement I made stabbed me with sharp, nauseating pain. Hunger and dehydration further weakened me. Worst of all, the drooling hyenas with blood on their faces waited to eat me, dead or alive. *I want daylight to come. I am so very tired. I refuse to be eaten alive. I refuse to be eaten alive …*

I could not imagine hyenas ripping my flesh with their razor-sharp teeth while I was still alive. I did not want to die a terrible, slow, and painful death. *Is this my last night on earth? Would my family recognize my remains, if the hyenas got to me? Are any of my family fighting for their lives tonight like I am? If my father were with me now, he would fight off these hyenas. I must not let my emotions weaken me. I must be strong and not let these merciless killers eat me alive. I must fight off these hyenas until my last breath. I am determined to live! I must live!*

The termite hill saved my life that night. I was grateful to be alive, but my struggle for life was far from finished.

Somehow, the longest night of my life ended, the sun rose, and the hyenas drifted away. Safe on the termite hill, I felt relieved that the night was over, but I did not know what to do next. My urine had run out, and I felt limp from thirst, hunger, fatigue, and throbbing pain. I looked around and saw no one, but I was not alone. My new companions were the vultures cleaning up after the hyenas. The vultures picked at places the hyenas could not reach. I looked away as they pulled eyes out of human faces. The merciless sun blazed on the termite hill and seared me. Though I tried to stay awake, I kept nodding off. I needed to risk the vultures to escape the sun.

Gasping in pain, I pushed myself down the termite hill and dragged myself to the shade of a nearby tree. This was cooler than being in the open on the hill. But the vultures, their heads covered in dried blood, wasted no time. They gathered around me when they realized that I was a weak and wounded human. They would eat me as soon as I died or became powerless. They sat and waited.

As they gathered around me and jostled one another, I imagined they were discussing which one would get to tear out my eyes. The bigger birds took the front row with the smaller ones behind, all waiting for me to die. Each time one of them took a step forward, the rest would follow. It was like a race, each vulture hoping to attack me first. Each time they got close to me, I swung my arm to scare them and show them I was still alive. Then the big ones would scare away the smaller ones, but they always came back.

How can this be happening to me? Why God, why? What have I done to deserve this? You saved my life from the Arabs who shot me. Again, you saved me from the killer hyenas. Now I'm fighting for my life against these vultures. It hurts just to think of them poking out my eyes while I'm still breathing. God, if you wanted me to die, you should have let that bullet end my life. I would not have played dead if I'd known that you were just saving me for the vultures. It would have been quicker for the Arabs to see me alive and just shoot a bullet through my head. You could have let the hyenas eat me—they are quicker than the vultures. Please, God do not let me die like this. Not like this, God. I did not know where God was, but I vowed I would not be eaten alive. Slower and slower, I swung my arm to beat off the vultures.

Chapter 10

Rescued

By now, news of the attack had reached Kuanylualthuan and Torpuot village, a day's walk away. My brother Duol worked as a nurse for the United Nations International Children's Emergency Fund (UNICEF) in Kuanylualthuan. He and my aunts in Torpuot had heard about the attack from those who fled. My sister and my cousin told them I had been shot. I later learned that my aunt had been shot, too. Luckily, the bullet had missed her bone and gone straight through her thigh. She had managed to escape with the help of her family. UNICEF sent boats to pick up the wounded who had managed to reach the river. My brother and another man drove the boat back and forth to Kuanylualthuan.

Shortly past noon, people started to look for missing family members and call their names. The greedy vultures flew to the tops of the nearby trees to keep watch. Nyatuach, a lady from my church and village, passed only seventy-five feet away. I tried to call, "Hello," but she could not hear me. My mouth was dried like concrete, and my lips cracked like dried land. My mouth felt sealed like a trap that could barely open.

"Hello. Hello." She walked further away. She was my only hope for survival. I could not make it through another terrifying night. *She must find me. God, she must find me. God, she must.*

As she began to disappear in the bushes and dried grass, I opened my mouth and felt my lips crack. With all my energy, I pushed my voice and screamed so loudly that the birds in the treetops flew off and the vultures backed away.

For three to five more minutes, I screamed, each effort shocking my nerves. My lips split, and tiny drops of blood dripped onto my shirt. Still the vultures watched, and the lady did not come. Finally, my desperate shrieks caught her attention. She recognized me, Gatluk the drummer boy from church.

Without a word, she handed me her metal water jug; then she pulled it away because I could not stop drinking. She sat with me, crying, helpless, and terrified by seeing me and not yet finding her two missing daughters. She asked me if I had seen them, but I had not. The disfigured dead were difficult to identify after the hyenas had gnawed their bodies and the vultures had pecked away eyes and faces.

"Please tell my parents I am wounded but still alive." I did not want her to leave me, but I did want her to find my parents.

"I will," she promised, her face blank with shock. While I waited for Nyatuach to carry my message, thoughts of losing my family tormented me. What if she could not find my parents? What if they all had died? What would happen to me if I had no family left? If she couldn't find my family, would she return to tell me? *I must not let my emotion get the best of me. I must believe everyone is okay.*

About three hours after Nyatuach left me with the vultures still waiting, my dad and uncle Jok finally found me. Both Dad and Jok carried two spears apiece. Now these hyenas and vultures would have no chance to eat me. I was protected.

Before my dad and uncle could speak, I saw my father cry for the first time in my life. His heart was broken. Two of his sons had died, and now the third one had just been shot. They did not know whether I would live.

Dad cried, so my uncle asked, "Where did you get shot?"

"On the hip."

"Is it broken?" asked uncle. I nodded in reply.

My uncle knew that trying to carry me with my arms around their necks would be too painful for me. He told my dad to stay with me while he searched for others to help carry me. Dad sat with tears rolling down his face.

"Dad, I'm not dead yet. I'm still alive," I said, trying to assure him I would be okay. I had never seen my strong father so helpless. I had always felt secure around him, and now he was broken down on his knees. Still, he was my dad, and just being beside him made me feel safe. Nyatuach had kept her promise, but I was never able to thank her. To this day, I do not know whether she found her daughters, dead or alive.

Just as dusk was falling, my uncle returned with two other men to help move me. They carried me to an empty village. My dad laid me in a deserted hut and then built a fire. He stayed with me through the night. Now I had water to drink. I wanted to sleep but could not because my leg had swollen so much. I kept asking my dad to turn me and give me water.

When the swelling reached my stomach, my body was hot to the touch, but I felt very cold. Dad kept the fire going to keep me warm, but I was in too much agony to sleep. Dad did not know what to do and did not sleep that night. Staring into the flames, I kept remembering the captain's speech: "Kill or be killed." *The Arabs got me. They shot me. Now I am going to die.*

Meanwhile, my uncle continued to search all night for more people who could carry me to the boat.

Once the sun rose, Dad brought me out of the hut, which had grown quite cold once the fire went out, for we had no blanket. My uncle Jok, my aunt Nyapauri's husband, and my mother returned with people who could carry me to the village. Mom tightened the sheet around her stomach and sat next to me. She placed my head in her lap and chanted over and over, "They shot you. They shot you. They shot you." Her tears covered my face, and she wailed, "God, what have I done? Why are you taking my children away from me? If I am the one you want, take me." She already blamed herself for the deaths of my two brothers. Now my life hung on the edge. She was sure I would die. I did not know how to comfort her.

To reach the boat on the Sobat River meant a half-day walk for those carrying me on a stretcher. We had not left until noon, so by the time we reached the river's edge, the boat had already left for Nasir (Kuanylualthuan). We spent the night, the third since I had been shot, near the river and waited for Duol to return with the boat the next morning around 10:00 a.m.

Mom spotted it first and stood on the bank waving. My brother Duol and his coworker made their way to where I was lying. Duol fought back tears. I had never before seen him burn with anger and pain like this. That day, he too feared losing a third brother. In my heart, I knew that he would not have left me when I was shot. He would have died protecting me.

Silently, he pulled back the sheet covering me and saw my swollen leg. Mom burst into fresh tears. My brother injected a high dose of painkiller into my right butt before they attempted to carry me to the boat. This would help me endure the three-hour boat trip to Kuanylualthuan.

Once we arrived in Kuanylualthuan, I was transported to the hospital, but they were not equipped to remove the bullet. I waited for four days to be taken to the hospital run by UNICEF. Meanwhile, I was given more doses of pain killers and antibiotics and had my wound dressed. That was all the hospital could do. The doctors would not operate because there was no surgical equipment.

On my third day in the hospital in Kuanylualthuan—six days since I had been shot—the doctor approached my family sitting by my bed to announce that due to the severity of my wound, I would go to Kenya for additional care. I had to go alone. A plane had arrived from Kenya to take me. He left and returned quickly with an injection of painkiller for the journey. Then I was rushed into a Toyota Land Cruiser waiting outside. The driver took off, and my family followed on foot to the airport about a mile away. At the airport, the plane was still being unloaded with medical supplies. My family arrived just as I was being transferred from the car and into the plane. Mom cried as I was brought on board; she was not permitted to go with me. I took a hard look at my family's faces, trying to memorize them. I prepared my final good-byes in case I never saw them again.

For the second time, I was going to be separated from my family—this time in a country far away. Would I see them again? Would I survive the trip? Severely wounded and only thirteen years old, I was again on my own.

Chapter 11

Intensive Care in Kenya

Though I had always dreamed of flying so I could look down from the sky, my first-ever flight found me lying on a stretcher, unable to see anything. I was on my way to Kenya. As soon as we landed a few hours later, I was taken to Lokichoggio Hospital for X-rays and surgery to remove the bullet in my hip. My family knew only that I had been flown to the United Nations hospital in Kenya. They had no way of learning about my condition.

Seven days later, I woke up from the anesthesia, my body full of pins and tubes. As I looked around the room and wondered where I was, I saw that the doctors had cut open my belly, and instead of putting my leg in a cast, they had drilled pins into it. Now my leg hung by cords over my bed. For the next seven months, I remained in intensive care and the bullet remained in my hip. The doctors said they could not remove the bullet right away because X-rays could not show where it was; it kept moving.

I shared the intensive-care unit with fifteen other patients. Nurses worked around the clock feeding us, changing our beds, dressing our wounds. I will never forget my nurses, Elizabeth and Philip. She would start on one side of the unit, and he would start on the other. Everyone liked Philip because he was so friendly and talked all the time, but drinking before his shifts caused problems.

One morning, Philip came to work to change dressings with Elizabeth. No one noticed anything different about Philip because it was often hard to tell when he had been drinking. I would not say he was drunk, but he probably had had more alcohol than normal. Patients complained that he was rougher than usual as he undressed and cleaned their wounds. To remove a soiled dressing, it is regular procedure to make sure the gauze is soft to prevent it sticking to the wound and tearing off new skin. That day, Philip ignored procedure and was not easy on me. After he removed the top layer of bandages, he started ripping at the gauze. I grabbed his hand to stop him from hurting me.

"Philip! That hurts! Soak the bandage!" I yelled in Nuer language.

Of course, Philip could not understand me because I could not speak English or the Kenyan language, Swahili. I tried to point at the sterile water for softening my crusty gauze. But Philip was not interested in either procedure or my pain and kept tearing off gauze. I could only read his determined body language and knew that he was not paying attention to me.

But the worst was yet to come.

Still not paying attention to me, Philip began to clean one of my wounds where a tube had been stitched in place just below my belly button. This allowed fluid to drain from stomach surgery. When Philip grasped this gauze with his pointed scissors, he caught the incision and tore it. I screamed and twisted in pain. Clearly flustered, Philip tried to shove the tube back into me.

"Stop! Stop!" I screamed and grabbed his hand to keep it away from me. "Elizabeth!"

She hurried to finish my care, and Philip was called to the office for disciplinary action. The surgeon determined that the damage needed surgery and the next day repaired the once-healing wound. Days of pain followed—all so unnecessary.

The next day, Philip came to me with Gatwech, a Nuer man working for the United Nations. He spoke some English and could translate for him.

"Sorry for what I done to you," Philip said through the interpreter. I looked at Philip and could tell he was really sorry, so I accepted his apology. We are still friends, but I never allowed Philip to change my dressings again.

Gentle Elizabeth, on the other hand, was so much more than a nurse to me. About thirty, she cared for me, not just as a patient but as though I were her own child. During those long months in intensive care, I tried to figure out how a woman from Kenya could open her heart to a boy from South Sudan. Other nurses treated me as a patient and then at the end of the day went home to their families, but Elizabeth always stopped by me when she arrived in the morning and when her shift ended in the evening. Maybe I just did not expect anyone to bother about me the way she did. I never came up with an answer, but I knew from her slow, soft English speech that she was a loving, warmhearted person. Except for my name spoken with an accent, I could understand her words only through an interpreter.

"You are going to be okay, Gatluk," she insisted. Her words gave me hope that I would get better and walk and return to my family and village in South Sudan.

"Does it hurt? Am I hurting you? Let me know if it hurts," Elizabeth always said when dressing my wounds. I nodded or shook my head as her words became familiar to me. Her kindness needed no translation. I wondered if she had kids of her own, but I never had the chance to ask her. If so, they are the luckiest kids in the world.

In spite of Elizabeth's care, I could not avoid the sadness in our unit. A kid my age, Makako, had the bed on my left, about four feet from mine. Through Gatweech, the interpreter, I learned that Arabs had set fire to his house, killing his entire family. Makako survived the fire covered from head to toe with severe burns. Sometimes he would emotionally break down and just cry and cry. Whenever someone asked him why he cried, he sobbed, "I have no family. I am the only one left." I could not imagine his physical or mental pain: everyone gone and no one awaiting his return. Then I began to worry whether my family would be killed while I was away. After that, I tried not to think about my family far away.

The bed to my right held a young mother and her four-month-old daughter. Both had been shot while she carried the baby in her arms. After a month in intensive care, the baby died, and the mother's tears were unstoppable. I was reminded of my own mother, whose heart had been broken so many times in her life. No one should outlive her children, yet war made it happen over and over again.

Another time, a pregnant woman was brought to intensive care many days after being shot in both legs. By the time she arrived, there was nothing the doctors could do. Ultimately, they decided to save the baby. The nurses named him Taban, which means "tired" or "close to death" in Arabic. They kept him at the hospital for eight months before sending him home to his father.

Two weeks after I arrived in Kenya, my uncle's wife, Nyakouth, was brought to the hospital. She had been shot in her left thigh. The bullet went straight through her flesh, missing bone, and her surgery was successful. Her arrival brought good news to me that my family was still alive. Our encounter was the first time any of my family had heard from me since I had left South Sudan three months earlier. All those months, my family had no idea where I was or if I was even alive. Now my family would have some hope that I would one day return home. When my aunt was flown back to Kuanylualthuan, she took these hopeful messages with her.

The entire seven months I had been in intensive care, I had not been able to feed myself due to my legs being elevated in traction and tubes in my belly; I could not sit up. Once I was able to feed myself, I was released from intensive care and taken to a building for independent patients. Surgeons checked wounds once a week, but nurses came daily to change dressings. For the most part, Philip and Elizabeth worked only in intensive care, yet Elizabeth visited me whenever she had a chance.

When the surgeons visited on Monday, their nurses also came to keep everything in order. Solomon was one of these nurses. His long, droopy mustache, like a walrus's, made him funny-looking. He never quite learned how to pronounce my name and always called me "Gatluak Gatluak," thinking my first name and my middle name the same. I never blamed him because Gatluk and Gatuak sound almost identical. After a while, he started calling me "Sudani," I guess because I was from Sudan and he had so much trouble with my real name. He was the one who wrote "OT," short for operation, above our heads when we had surgery in the morning and needed to fast.

Even at the hospital, food was in short supply. If someone I knew was scheduled for an operation, it was the golden opportunity for an extra meal for me because that patient had to fast. To get his food, I had to erase the OT from the board above his bed. Otherwise, the orderly would know not to leave the food. It wasn't very good, but it was something.

Patients always complained about the food. For breakfast, we had cornmeal or tea. For lunch, we had red kidney beans and corn flour mixed together like mashed potatoes. Dinner was the same as lunch plus rice and canned sardines or, once a week, meat. Soup tasted like a bowl of water.

One man in my building decided to protest the watery soup and threw it against the front of the building. He managed to convince about half the building to do the same, hoping to draw attention. He even stopped the workers from cleaning it off the walkway because he wanted the director to see his protest. The director was not happy with his story and told the food manager that those who wasted their food would not receive food for seven days.

Yes, he carried out his threat.

Two months after I arrived in Kenya, the Arabs reclaimed Kuanylualthuan and chased the SPLA to a village called Mading, a day-and-a-half walk away. Once the SPLA established a post there and cleared land for an airstrip, the United Nations began to fly from Mading, and many more people were airlifted to the hospital in Kenya.

My cousin Gatwech was brought to the hospital with three gunshot wounds: one to the thigh, one to the left shoulder, and one to the right wrist that broke both bones in his arm. Three months later, his younger brother Reath arrived at the hospital with a snake bite in his left wrist. Because it had been untreated for two months, the poison had destroyed the muscles between his wrist and elbow. The doctor had to amputate his arm above the elbow to save his life. Just six weeks later, he returned to Mading. I asked him to tell my family that I was still alive, if he saw them, but he did not know where they were. Gatwech and I remained at the hospital. At least we could see each other every day and eat together. He was all the family I had.

Chapter 12

I Relearn to Walk

Over the next eight months, doctors tried several times to remove the bullet in my hip. Each time the bullet would not be where it had been on the X-ray. The doctors told me that because my bones and muscles were growing rapidly, the bullet was traveling with that growth. After I had been in the hospital for eleven months, the bullet was finally removed, and the swelling in my leg began to go down. Now I was ready to begin physical therapy, the painful process that would help me to walk again.

Every evening, Daniel, the short, chubby therapist, wheeled me in a wheelchair to the therapy building, where he began by rubbing my leg with a bar of ice shaped like a bar of soap. Then he massaged my leg. After that, he would exercise my leg, pushing my foot back and forth and flexing my knee to increase my range of motion. All these movements hurt me. Pain medication and Daniel's constant smiles helped only a little. I began to dread physical therapy and saw Daniel not as the person who would help me walk, but as one who caused me pain.

After two weeks of this, I still could not take even a single step because I was so weak from twelve months in a hospital bed and wheelchair. Daniel helped me to stand, light-headed and shaking, gripping two rails on either side of me. I could only stand on my weak "good" leg; my weaker, skinny leg could not support me. Daniel eased me down into the wheelchair after a couple of seconds. Then we tried again. Each day, I stood a little bit longer. Four weeks after starting physical therapy, I could stand for more than two minutes without shaking or feeling dizzy. Still, I did not like to see Daniel because he always caused me pain.

Then, in the fifth week of therapy, after thirteen months in the hospital, I took my first step. That was my turning point. After being confined to a hospital bed and wheelchair for over a year, I could taste freedom. Now I knew that with time and courage, I could walk again. Now I saw Daniel as someone who truly wanted to help me to walk, not as someone who inflicted pain for nothing. He walked alongside me as I grasped the rails and hopped on my good right leg, but I still had to put weight on my left leg.

Once I gained more strength and balance, I was put on the walker. I no longer needed to depend on the wheelchair to get around. The same day that Daniel gave me the walker, I walked myself into the shower room and took my first real shower after over a year of sponge baths. Refreshed and independent, I felt full of hope.

After three weeks of walking with the walker, eight weeks since I had started physical therapy, the swelling continued to decrease as strength in my arms and right leg increased. Daniel instructed me to tiptoe weight-bearing on my left leg. By week ten of physical therapy, Daniel put me on crutches. My balance was off, and I almost fell, but with a few tries, I was good to go.

After a year and three months in the hospital and eleven weeks in physical therapy, my hip had healed but fused closed. The damage could not be repaired, so my femur fused to my pelvis as a single bone instead of being able to flex and swivel. Both the fused hip and severe nerve damage created my permanent limp—a limp that would remind me forever what had happened that terrible day.

Elizabeth still came by whenever she could. Daniel continued to see me, rub my leg with ice, massage it, and help me exercise without equipment to build strength. The severe nerve damage in my leg meant I could not gain strength fast. Even so, Daniel coached me to half weight-bearing on the leg. He came by a couple of times a week to take me for a walk and evaluate my progress. Crutches made me feel so free after dealing with the slow walker. Now I had freedom to move.

Three weeks later, Daniel instructed me in full-weight bearing. My leg was still weak and painful. As much as I wanted to walk without crutches, after a year of not walking, I was not ready to let go of them. My left leg was much skinnier, and even when I used two crutches, it wobbled when

I tried to stand on it. I realized that I would never walk normally again. I had to accept that the limp would be part of my life. I had no choice. I had to live with it.

During the day, Gatwech, our friend Muoch, and I played traditional games in the shade of trees. I learned how to play dominoes by watching Gatwech play with other people there. I also started to learn Arabic. Each day, I picked up a few new words from random conversations. I learned a lot from a man named Deng, whom I met after I was discharged from intensive care to the independent patient building. His bed was next to mine. Deng was from the Dinka tribe in South Sudan and spoke Arabic whenever his friends came to see him.

For instance, his friends greeted him, *"As-Salaam-Alaikum,"* meaning, "Unto you, peace."

Deng replied, *"Wa-Alaikum-Salaam,"* meaning, "And unto you, peace."

Gatwech stayed in the hospital for a full year before completing his treatment. When he was discharged, he moved to a separate building for people awaiting flights home. Patients could choose to return where they had come from or to go to the United Nations' Kakuma Refugee Camp in Kenya. Gatwech chose his village in South Sudan instead of the refugee camp, was put on a waiting list, and flew back to Mading five weeks later. He would then walk four hours to his village.

"I will try to find your family and let them know you are still alive," he promised right before boarding the Isuzu truck for the airport. I did not let my emotions show and just nodded my head for an okay. That was our last conversation.

Five months after Gatwech left, I was discharged and had a week to decide where to go. After seventeen months in Kenya, I was not sure I was ready to risk returning to my village, since I did not even know where my family was. The refugee camp was appealing because there would be safety and less chance of attack, but I would be completely on my own. On the other hand, South Sudan was still a war zone. People died every day, and vultures fed on human remains. This was one of the toughest decisions I have ever had to make. Ultimately, I decided to go home to South Sudan and find my family. I prayed, "God, let my family know that I will be coming home soon, if they are still alive. Could you have a family member waiting for me in Mading when I arrive? That would be great."

When my name reached the top of the list on the bulletin board outside the building, I started to question my decision. *Did I make the right choice to return to South Sudan? What will happen to me if my family is dead? On the other hand, I have waited a long time for this day to come. I will not change my mind.*

I was so excited to go home after being away for almost a year and a half. Yet I worried whether I could make it on crutches from Mading along the cracked earth trail. Sometimes the trail could be mud. For the strong, this was a two-day walk; for me, it would take a week. Plus, there was no guarantee that I would find my family. Doubts sat with me like vultures, just waiting to peck at me like when I had been shot. I would not give up then. I would not give up now. All I could do was try not to think too much and hope that everything would work out.

My brother Ngut found out that I had been shot while he lived in the refugee camp in Ethiopia. When he learned that I still had not returned after a year and a half, he decided to go home to find out what was going on. If my family had heard nothing, he would cross from Ethiopia into Kenya and look in the only two places I could be: The United Nations hospital in Lokichogio, the only place the United Nations would bring patients from South Sudan, and the Kakuma Refugee Camp, the only choice for discharged patients who chose not to return home.

Our aunts in Ethiopia told him that my family still lived in the same village. They had stayed so I could find them when I returned. Their hopes paid off when Ngut arrived from Ethiopia. He shared his plan with my parents. He would walk to Mading to find out what he could about me. He left on a Thursday night and planned to arrive Friday night.

Meanwhile, that Friday morning, along with other discharged patients returning to South Sudan, I headed by car to the Lokichogio airport. Rainy season storms delayed our flight until 1:00 p.m., when we finally made our way onto the little jet with ten or fifteen seats. Center seats had been removed to make room for medical supplies. I sat on the floor by the windows and watched as we soared over the villages.

On my first flight, I had been so drugged and in pain, I had missed this view, so different from anything I had ever seen before. Smoke rose from cattle camps. Barns and huts looked like small doghouses from up here. As our plane started to go lower as we got closer to Mading, I saw men herding cattle down to the Sobat River to drink water. I saw women carrying pots of water back to the village on a tiny footpath. I saw men clearing wheat in the farm fields. These sights from the little airplane window could not compare with vistas I had seen as a boy looking down from the tops of trees I climbed. I did not want the ride in the sky to end.

Soon, we tilted and turned toward the Mading airstrip, and a man by the runway with a bag on his back caught my attention. Something about him seemed very familiar. The pilot made another turn and landed the plane safely on the uneven dirt runway. I thought the wings would break from the shaking. The door opened, and I gripped the two rails on either side of the five stairs and inched my way down carrying only the white sack I had made in the army. It held my one blanket. I held my crutches. These were my only possessions besides the clothes I wore.

Again, I glimpsed the man with the bag approaching the plane, but he was too far away for me to recognize him. We passengers were led to an abandoned house to sit and wait.

Chapter 13

"God Threw You Back"

After hours on the plane, I was in no mood for more sitting, so I stood outside. I kept thinking about the man by the runway and wondered why he stayed in my mind. Just as I was about to go back inside the hut, someone called, "Gatluk!" I immediately recognized the voice. Ngut! My brother! As soon as I turned around, I saw the man with the bag on his back lunging toward me.

I thought I was dreaming and could not believe my luck. No, this was not luck. God had answered my prayer. Ngut and I hugged, silent but filled with happy emotion. I fought the tears that wanted to fall down my cheeks. Not only was I excited that we were reunited, but I was also glad I had not chickened out on my decision to return home to South Sudan. Neither of us had expected anything like this.

Inside the hut, I introduced Ngut to the people from the plane, who asked him questions about their families in Ethiopia. Since he had just arrived, he didn't have much to tell. I could not wait to ask my big, scary question and feared the answer: "Ngut, where is our family?"

"They are still living in our home in our village, Muon."

"All of them, Ngut?"

"Yes. All of them."

Safe! Now I could breathe. The dread that had weighted me down for a year and a half lifted from my shoulders.

A man in a green uniform approached and asked if any of us knew people there in Mading. I told him I knew a man named Gatwech. The man in uniform knew my cousin and said he would see if Gatwech were still around. He often came to Mading to try to get his UNICEF nursing job back.

A few minutes later, Gatwech arrived. *"Male jiduol!"* (This means, "Hello, people at the house.") Now I felt even better. Seeing him reminded me that I was not alone anymore. Gatwech suggested that we go to a cattle camp where his family was staying, a three- or four-hour walk away. Meanwhile, Ngut would walk back to our village, a much longer journey, to tell our parents the amazing news of my arrival.

"Jali ka mal," I said—"Travel in peace." After goodbyes, Gatwech and I slowly made our way to the cattle camp. The foot trail was muddy, and my crutches would stick in it, making my arms tired. We stopped every now and then to rest my arms. Walking with crutches was harder than I thought, so the trip took five hours. I stayed with my cousin and his family and waited until my parents could come.

One day, I was lying in the men's hut when I heard two gunshots and a lady singing outside. I had no idea what was going on and thought, *Perhaps this is how Gatwech's relatives welcome him home from Kenya.* But the singing lady was not there for Gatwech—she was there for me.

My brother Duol had fired the shots, and my mother sang a made-up song for joy. By the time I limped outside on my crutches, I saw the whole neighborhood watch this strange woman singing her heart out through her happy tears. I dropped my crutches and hugged my brother. I gave my mom my head to spit on. I had no words to express my happiness.

Limp with relief, Mom kept singing and sat on a dried cow skin on the ground with her legs out straight in front of her. She told me to sit in her lap, but I did not want to. At fourteen year old and nearly six feet tall, I was much too old to sit on my mother's lap, but she insisted, and I did not want to disappoint her. Then she held my head to her bosom and called me all the pet names she had called me as a baby: *Chanyod* ("do not touch"), *Gatnor* ("baby palm tree") and *Lukmaan* ("woman judge"). "You came back alive! You came back alive! All this time you been gone, I did not know if you had died or were still alive. God of heaven threw you up. He threw you back to me!" I just sat and listened to my mother rejoice. Through those many months, Mom feared she had lost me along with her sons Tut and Gatdet. Now her despair lifted. To her, I had essentially come back from the dead.

Though, I, too, was overwhelmed with happiness, I would not show it with tears. I did not want to embarrass myself and make those around me think I was weak. Even my mother would have been embarrassed if I cried. Outside, I remained emotionless, but inside, I was dying to cry.

Six weeks, later we had to leave the cattle camp. Gatwech had been able to get his United Nations nursing job back, but we had to relocate to Mading, three or four hours away on foot, to be close enough. In preparation for the move, he started building a compound in Mading. All but the barn roof was finished when we moved in with his family. Everyone helped to finish the barn roof, which is made of long, dried grasses stacked together on top of the wood frame to block rain and mosquitoes.

Now the weather changed. The Sobat River always flooded during the rainy season, filling up all the low land the waters could reach. This made walking on foot difficult, as the canals would overflow. We had no choice but to wait in Mading until the dry season came.

Before it was possible to see the rest of my family, my leg began to hurt. My left calf and foot swelled so much that my skin and calf muscle split open. It would not get better. Within four months of our arrival in Mading, the pain became so bad that the clinic staff decided I needed to be taken back to the United Nations hospital in Lokichogtio, Kenya, for more treatment. This was the only hospital that would take South Sudanese patients for free medical care. But after spending seventeen months at the United Nations hospital, I did not want to go back. Besides, I was determined not to leave my mother again. I would not put her through more heartache, wondering whether I was alive. No. *If I am going to die, then I will die here. At least my mother will know where I am buried. But if God did not mean for that bullet to kill me, then I will not die—and I want to be with my mother.* This time, I had a choice.

Two days later, a plane came for me. I asked the medic, "Will my mother be coming with me?"

He wasn't sure. "Have her accompany us to the airport, and we'll find out."

It turned out that United Nations policy allowed only patients who needed treatment to be flown to Kenya. My mother could not come. I could tell that she was disappointed.

"I refuse to go without her."

"Then there is nothing we can do for you. Let us know if you change your mind."

I could tell from my mother's body language that she was upset I refused treatment. I still had the option to change my mind, but there was no way I would leave my mother again. I thought I could handle pain better than separation.

Chapter 14

Dark Thoughts

As the months went on, my leg pain became unbearable. I could not sleep at night or even during the day. Painkillers from the United Nations clinic in Mading offered some relief, but could not control it. Still, I refused to change my mind and leave my mother behind to seek hospital care in Kenya. *God, take my life or take my pain if I am not going to die. God, you must put an end to this. I cannot go on.* Dark thoughts began to creep into my mind like soft-footed jungle cats.

After three months, the nonstop pain made my stress nonstop as well. I became quieter and mentally isolated myself. More and more, I found myself in a small, dark corner of my head, lost in ugly thoughts. I was so good at hiding my feelings that not even my mother could suspect my dark plan.

Suicide.

I had convinced myself that death was the only way to stop the pain. Not death by being a boy soldier or death from Arabs or death from being mauled by hyenas or vultures. No. I could die by my own hand. I was so lost in suicide thoughts that I never stopped to consider returning to Kenya without my mother. During the day, whenever I sat alone in the barn, I stared at my cousin's AK-47 on the wall and thought about ending the pain forever. How should I stand? Would I die quicker by a bullet to the brain or to the heart?

Before I could decide, someone would come into the barn and disrupt my dismal thoughts. I would feel burning anger at the interruption, but showed no emotion on my face. No one knew. These dark thoughts came in waves, some days worse than others.

By the time the dry season finally came, my wounds had begun to heal. I began to feel a bit better as the sun became hotter each day. Many people, including my mom, would say that people who had been shot felt pain during the wet season—sometimes for years—after their wounds healed. Though I still felt pain, I managed without the painkillers, my stress eased, and I no longer thought about killing myself. I was coming back to life, but things were dying around me. After my sister Nyadiew's husband visited, the cow and calf they had given to me both died from some unknown disease as the dry season began in earnest.

Now water was far away and harder to find. People traveled a few miles each day just to collect enough for drinking, cooking, and bathing. My brother-in-law went on to visit my father, who asked him to find men to carry me back to our village. In Nuer tradition, a man cannot carry his brother-in-law, so he found two men who, along with his two brothers, carried me on a stretcher from Mading to my village. Being carried for two full days reminded me of when I had been shot and had to be carried to the Sobat River. I tried not to remember.

Finally, my family was nearly whole again, except for Ngut, who went back to the refugee camp in Ethiopia. He feared that if he stayed with us, he could be recruited by the SPLA army. We had new family additions: Duol's little girl, the first grandchild for my parents, who had been born four months after I had been taken to Kenya, and my sister's little girl, born two years after I returned from Kenya. I always enjoyed holding them and being an uncle when I had the chance.

During the seventeen months I had been in the hospital, all of my peers had received their manhood marks, the Nuer ceremonial forehead scarring that initiates a boy's passage to manhood. With these marks come responsibility and respect. Since I had missed this important ritual, I had been excluded from my peers. I could not even say *"Maa"* to those younger than me if they had their manhood marks. *"Maa"* is a term used among peers who receive their manhood marks in the same year, as well as by older men in reference to younger men.

Once, while looking for a loose cow, I called a young man I knew *"Maa"* because he was younger than me. He turned on me and wanted to fight; he had manhood marks, and I didn't. After that, all I could think about was getting my manhood marks. Some girls would not even talk to me because I did not have my marks yet. At dances, girls would go so far as to run their hands over men's faces before agreeing to dance, to be sure their partner was a man and not just a boy. I felt enormous relief when I got my manhood marks that year.

At the end of the dry season, I left South Sudan to be with Ngut in Ethiopia. My parents thought it would be better for me to be near a hospital, even a small one, in case my leg started to bother me again. I knew I would be safer, but I hated to leave my parents behind, especially my mom, who could not bring me to Ethiopia because she was sick with diarrhea and internal bleeding. The walk to the border is normally a three-day journey, but because of my injury, my Aunt Nyanguda and I took a full seven days to reach Ethiopia. My leg was so sore, and it took two weeks for the swelling to go down.

My aunt did not live at the refugee camp, so she sent a message to let Ngut know of my arrival. I also saw Wal again. I had not seen him since we started running that day I was shot, three and a half years ago. Soon, Duol and his family arrived in Ethiopia with their new baby boy. My brother now worked with a Nuer doctor he had met when our mother was sick. I felt relieved to stay with my brother and his young family.

Because there was little for me to do, I walked around the city when I grew bored. That's how I met Kueth, a man who made his living by walking around Gambela selling bananas. He was only three or four years older than I. When I told him I had nothing to do and that I was interested in selling bananas, he showed me where I could buy my own to sell. He also agreed to teach me what he knew of the business. I had enough money left from what my brother had given to me to start. The next day, Kueth took me to the banana seller and was kind enough to let me walk with him as we sold the fruit. We sold them all. From that day on, we sold our bananas together.

One day, when Kueth was not feeling well, I went out to sell bananas on my own. During my walk, I saw some boys gathered by the sidewalk, so I moved closer. The boy in the middle displayed three cards, two red and one black, before turning them face down and shuffling them around.

Every so often, he would show the fronts of the cards to the audience, but he kept rearranging them. During all of this, he took bets from people who thought they could identify the black card at the end of the game. Just before it was over, he started moving the cards very fast to confuse everyone. Then he put them face down and offered the money in his hand, sometimes five, ten, twenty, and even fifty birr to anyone who could identify the winning card. Some won. Some lost. I bet twice and lost nine birr. I was disappointed that I didn't win, but I soon learned that for some, losing was more than a disappointment.

I walked away, ticked off after losing, and met a woman sitting on a stone not far from the gambling site. She had lost more than three hundred birr trying to win back the money she had lost and started to cry when she realized all her money was gone. She told me that she had just moved from Lare with her husband to live here with his family. He had sold one of his cows and had given her the money to buy clothes for herself and food for the family. When she came across the boys gambling, she thought she could have yet more money and took a chance. Then another and another. Now she would have to face her husband empty-handed.

I wondered what she would tell him. Would she tell him this truth about gambling for money, or would she lie and say she had been robbed? The city was full of pickpockets, so it could be a believable story, but she would be lying to her new family. Hearing her talk made me glad I did not have to report my losses to anyone.

After walking around the city selling bananas for a couple of weeks, my leg could no longer take the strain. To earn money, I started selling grilled sweet corn because I could sit by the bridge after sunrise, wait for customers, and not walk so much. I bought the corn for half a birr each from farmers who brought it from the countryside. Then I sold the grilled ears for one birr each. Staying in one place was easier on my leg, and I earned twenty-five to thirty birr each day. I decided to reward myself with a new shirt and some shorts because I had been wearing my old clothes for a year and a half.

When Ngut came from the refugee camp, I was thrilled. We had last seen each other two years earlier, in 1995, when I had returned from the hospital in Kenya. Ngut brought with him an SPLA veteran, Gatluak Taop, who had fought the Arabs in Kuanylualthuan. He was known as

Gatluak Nyaluok because he named himself after his mother, Nyaluok. Gatluak Nyaluok, a real "people person," was always surrounded by his many friends, whom he drew with his positive attitude. "I am Gatluak Nyaluok. I dance between sky and earth," he used to say.

Even with a leg amputated below the knee, his good nature had survived the horrors of war. A land mine had blown off his foot when his unit captain had forced him to lead the unit at night. Now he wore a yellow plastic prosthetic leg. About the only thing that ever made him mad was when people disrespected his sacrifice and made fun of his yellow leg.

One day, Gatluak got into an argument while playing dominoes in camp. The argument escalated and a man insulted Gatluak. "Yellow leg, you talk like you know everything, but if it comes to a fight, you would not do anything!" The man had foolishly underestimated Gatluak, assuming he was just a weak, one-legged man. Gatluak was mad. The crowd was silent. Everyone expected a fight at any moment.

Without a word, Gatluak lunged across the table and grabbed the man's shirt. With his other hand, he punched the man in the face, breaking his teeth and his nose. Gatluak would have swung again, but an onlooker grabbed his arm. The disrespectful man was out cold, and with that, the fight was over. It seems true what people say about men who run their mouths: "Those who like to talk turn their actions in words; those who like to stay quiet turn their words into actions." This man learned his lesson and never picked on Gatluak again. He was so ashamed that he had been so easily beaten by a one-legged man.

The day after Ngut and Gatluak arrived in Gambela, they went to the flea market to buy tobacco in order to resell it at a profit in the refugee camp. They had been doing this for years because there was so much money to be made. Gatluak returned to camp about a week ahead of Ngut and me. As soon as we arrived in the camp, Ngut took me to the United Nations office in order to register to receive food, but I was refused. United Nations policy would not allow individual persons to be registered alone. I had to wait for more refugees to come to the camp to be tallied with me. Without the United Nations ration card, I was also forbidden to enroll in school.

While I waited to be enrolled, I depended on Ngut's ration, and the money he earned selling tobacco, for food. We shared a hut with two other men who were his friends. After a couple of months of waiting, more than a hundred refugees came to the camp, and I was registered to receive food and enroll in school.

I first attended school—at second-grade level—when I was about seventeen years old. Just before school started, I had learned from a friend how to say and write ABCs on paper with a pencil. I could hardly write my name, and I could not read, but I was not the only seventeen-year-old who did not know these things. I asked my new friend Bichiok, a friend of Ngut's, to give me reading lessons. He provided repetition so I could say most one-vowel words: dog, cat, cow, boy, girl. By the end of first semester, I finished third in the top ten of the students. Then, halfway into the second semester, my leg started to hurt from walking three miles each way to school. Once I was there, the aching pain made concentration on my schoolwork too difficult. I tried to push myself to keep attending classes, but the pain was too severe. I had no choice but to stop and resume the following school year.

With nothing to do most of the day, I found myself looking for something to sell, as I had done so many times before. Ngut and Gatluak sometimes asked me to help at the tobacco shop by preparing the plastic bags for customers' tobacco. In no time, I shared the shop with them and became a partner. Along with tobacco, I also sold oil, candles, beans, candies, soaps, and matches. Most people were not interested in selling these items because it was a slow business with little profit. But I am patient, and it was better than nothing.

Chapter 15

Lost Homeland and New Hope

Life was hard at the Dimma Refugee Camp, an emergency compound of tens of thousands of makeshift neighborhoods in Gambela region, a sunbaked region where temperatures rose to 104 degrees Fahrenheit. I shared my shelter with my brother Ngut and our three friends, Chuol, Duoth, and Gatluak. We entirely depended upon the United Nations for food and drinking water. As for the toilet, we just used the bushes.

A refugee camp should be a safe haven for those made homeless by the violence and destruction of civil war. With shelter and food, refugees should feel safe and feel that they have left the horror of their war-stricken lives behind them. Yet all of us at Dimma Camp still feared violence and hunger. The wilderness location in a tribal territory of Ethiopia left Dimma Camp not only undersupplied but in danger of tribal attacks, wild animals, and poisonous snakes and spiders. With little support from the United Nations and no protection from the Ethiopian government, we were on our own.

Months upon months would pass without anything from the United Nations. When food finally did arrive, there was never enough. A two-week supply for a single person consisted of one cup of white beans, one cup of oil, and one fifteen-inch can of sorghum grain, plus one bar of soap once a month. If we were careful to eat only one small meal a day, we could stretch those rations to last seven days. Eating two meals a day would use up rations in just four days. Many people routinely had to go without food for days, or sometimes weeks, at a time. The rainy season made things even worse because the United Nations food convoy would be further delayed by impassable roads. Much later, I learned that in our camp, thirty people a day had died.

Collecting and selling firewood was about the only way to make money to buy food at the stores owned by the Ethiopian traders in the main Dimma town while we waited for the United Nations. There we bought corn, flour, white beans, and oil. However, the tribes called Thurma living in the jungle around the camp brutally attacked people collecting firewood. If caught, men would be beaten to death and women would be raped and then killed. Danger was very real, but hunger drove people to take extreme risks. Reporting attacks to the United Nations was pointless, for even when children were kidnapped, reports accomplished nothing.

One time, my friend Kim and three other men were cutting trees to build a new hut when men from the forest tribe suddenly surrounded them, tied their hands behind them, and beat them. They managed to run to escape being beaten to death. During the chase, two were stepped on and stabbed, but they outran the killers to escape with their lives.

When they returned to camp, we were terrified to see those two covered in blood. One had been stabbed on his lower back and the other on his right shoulder. They were rushed to the United Nations hospital, where both recovered from their wounds.

The attack scared some people enough that they stopped collecting firewood, but for most, the certainty of hunger outweighed the risk of danger. It was difficult to decide whether the camp was safer than returning to South Sudan, but it didn't matter. The United Nations restricted who could leave the camp and never gave any reasons. This restriction resulted in the death of a girl I knew who was not allowed to leave camp and seek treatment in Addis Ababa.

For two years, I lived a life without hope or dreams in the Dimma Refugee Camp.

What little news came from South Sudan was never good: no end to the war in sight. In our isolated little camp, our only connection to the rest of the world was through the United Nations. We depended on the United Nations for food and protection, but they let us down. The two years I lived there, just scraping by, felt like decades.

Years before arriving at Dimma Camp in Ethiopia, I had heard stories of men who followed the Lost Boys' footsteps through the jungle to Kakuma (literally "nowhere") Camp, in order to cross into Kenya, 375 miles away. In Kenya, the International Organization for Migration (IOM) was granting political asylum (PA) to Sudanese refugees and sending them to places like Australia, Canada, and the United States of America. The possibility of finding a better life somewhere far away drove men to terrible risks: being eaten by animals or dying of dehydration or hunger. Hope fueled their journey through the jungle to find the IOM Kakuma Camp in Kenya.

One evening in the Dimma camp, people saw fourteen IOM workers enter the United Nations compound in a convoy of five Toyota Land Cruisers. Word quickly spread, and everyone hoped they had forms for political asylum (PA). The next day, we learned that they had come with PA forms to go to the United States—but only for certain people. The IOM wanted high school graduates. This upset a lot of people, as barely 1 percent of the refugees at Dimma had diplomas.

I, myself, had only a second-grade education, so my chances were slim at best. Because there were so few twelfth graders, hundreds of forms remained after the graduates applied. Then the IOM started taking applications from anyone—first come, first served. People at the front of the lines grabbed forms for themselves and all their relatives. Ngut tried to squeeze in to get forms, but there were not enough. We were out of luck.

When the forms ran out, I felt that the rest of us had missed a once-in-a-lifetime chance at a better life. But after everything that had already happened to me, I knew better than to give up hope. Maybe I was not meant to receive a form. Maybe that was for a reason.

A few days later, Ngut came to the shop to give me a blank piece of paper. The IOM was still at the camp conducting interviews of the people who were able to apply for political asylum in the United States. Ngut told me to bring the paper to Gatluak Wal, an educated man with a master's degree. He could write a letter on my behalf, explaining my medical condition and need for further treatment. By this time, I was still on crutches, and my leg hurt because my growing legs were uneven. My healthy right leg was three and a half centimeters longer than my left leg, which had muscle and nerve damage. Meanwhile, I continued to grow.

I found Gatluak listening to the radio in his compound. When I made my presence known, he greeted me as *Jesh-Ameer* ("Red Army" or child soldier). The Arab term had become popular among South Sudanese in the refugee camp after the rise of child soldiers in our homeland. He invited me to sit. I explained that I had come so that he could write a letter for me in hopes that my condition would help secure a form from the IOM.

He turned down the radio and asked, "What exactly would you want me to write?"

In our beautiful Nuer language, I explained what I wanted. Then with the radio still talking in the background, he began to write in clear, neat handwriting:

> To whom it may concern:
>
> My name is Gatluk Gatluak Digiew. I was wounded in the civil war in South Sudan on my left hip and need further treatment. Please, it would be a great opportunity to go to the United States of America to receive further treatment.
>
> Sincerely,
> Signed, Gatluk G. Digiew

This short letter took him less than two minutes to write from start to finish. On my way to the United Nations office later that evening, I began to doubt the effectiveness of a letter so brief. Was it enough of an explanation of my condition to convince IOM to consider me for political asylum? When he handed me the letter, Gatluak told me, "It's good to keep it short." *But not this short,* I thought. Surely, it should have been at least half a page to do any good. With a metal crutch in my right hand and the letter that would change my life in the other, I made my way to the office.

Thoughts of actually going to the United States hit me. *If I make it to the US, I could get my leg fixed. I would walk again without crutches.* To tell you the truth, I did not know anything about the United States except for seeing "USA" printed on the back of food sacks used to feed us. I heard people talk about how great America was. Everyone had a car, a house full of food, good clothes, and money, they said. Such were the pictures I painted in my head. But even more than all these wonderful things, all I wanted was to get my leg fixed. I wanted to be pain-free and walk again. That was all I wanted. I would put my hope and trust in God.

When I arrived at the United Nations office, I met Wech a family friend who lived with us in the camp.

"What are you doing here?"

"I'm here to give this letter to Shannon, the head of the IOM staff," I said raising the letter in my left hand.

Wech knew a little English. "Would you speak to us?" he asked Shannon in her language.

"The office is closed," said Shannon. "Please come back tomorrow."

"I only want to give you this letter," said my friend who pointed to me. "He wrote it for you."

Shannon took the letter, put it in her bag without opening it, and walked away.

I was wary of getting my hopes up, but kept my fingers crossed that night. By the next morning, I had completely forgotten about the letter. I don't know what distracted me. Maybe I thought that after the IOM gave out all the PA forms, nothing was left. Perhaps I did not want to have high hopes disappointed. Ngut suggested that I check, so I went back to the United Nations office, just in case.

People were gathered outside the office. I heard my name called just as I arrived. The interpreter knew who I was and had sent a man to find me. I met the man halfway, and together we walked to the office, but my leg dragged and kept me from moving very fast. I remember breathing heavily as we climbed a small hill, but I made it. In the office, Shannon was waiting for me.

Through the interpreter who spoke Nuer to me and English to her, she asked questions and wrote my answers on the form. When she asked about my relatives, I told her about Ngut. He had followed me to the office and was now called in from the crowd. Because he was older than me, his name was added to the top of the form. Just like that, a miracle! Our journey to the United States had begun—and we could not imagine what the place even looked like.

More than two months passed before we heard again from the IOM, and people were starting to worry. Ngut and I started to feel bad that we had not added Wech to our form. He was like a brother to us. Leaving him behind would mean that we were thinking only of ourselves because he was not a biological brother. Plus we worried about him. With no family to turn to, we were all he had. It would not be right to leave him in Ethiopia.

People warned us that adding Wech to our application could be very risky, and we could all be denied. I did not want to jeopardize this once-in-a-lifetime opportunity, but family in any form is always worth protecting. We decided to take our chances.

The IOM workers arrived ten weeks later to conduct follow-up interviews, which took three weeks. We were asked many questions. For example, "When did you come to the refugee camp? How long have you lived in the refugee camp? How many huts did your family have? How many sheep and cows did you family have before seeking refuge in the refugee camp?" Then we had our photos taken.

During our interview, Ngut asked if Wech could be added to the application. To our surprise, he was allowed. We gave him Tut's name in honor of our brother who passed away. For me, it was like seeing Tut come back to life.

Medical checkups came two months later. By now, it had been almost two years since I had arrived in Dimma. We were taken to the city of Jima, Ethiopia, to have blood drawn for tests. The doctors had a difficult time drawing blood because we were all so skinny. When the medical examinations were over, we were supposed to return to the camp. Ngut and I were left behind because the camp president had conflicts with Ngut back at the camp.

Actually, the camp president had problems with a lot of people in the camp because of how he mistreated them. Ngut was one of those who disagreed with him—and was beaten by the president's appointed police. (Eventually, the camp president's mistreatments caught up with him: a group of angry men beat him with sticks the size of baseball bats. He escaped with a broken left forearm.)

Because I was Ngut's brother, the bus ticket I had been given due to my injuries was confiscated. Ngut could not ride the trucks with the other men. Instead, we found a commercial bus that took us to a small town outside Mizan; we needed a connecting bus into Mizan itself. We waited at the bus station and boarded with the other passengers, but there were not enough seats. The Ethiopian man left standing demanded that the bus driver make one of the "foreigners" get off.

Ngut understood Amharic and told me the bus driver told the man to wait for the next bus because we had paid for our seats like everyone else. The man was furious and refused to wait. As an Ethiopian, he demanded the he be given preference over outsiders. All eyes turned to us. They looked at us as aliens who did not belong there. This was straight racial discrimination. The demanding Ethiopian did not point to any of the other people in the bus to get off because they were Ethiopian. He singled us out because we were foreigners, something that would never happen if we were in South Sudan.

We looked at the bus driver to see what he would do, as he was in control of the bus, but he was not on our side, after all. He did not want to be unpatriotic by taking strangers over a countryman and told one of us to leave. Ngut got off the bus. Then the other Ethiopian men on the bus laughed and pointed at me. I did not know what they were saying and assumed that they were cursing and making fun of me. I put my head down and tried not to look at them for the rest of the ride.

I learned an important lesson that day. Your homeland is your home, even if you walk naked and eat dirt. When you are in your country, you can get away with a lot more than you can as an outsider. I was reminded why I was in Ethiopia to begin with: my countrymen were fighting and dying to have a country to call home. It hurt to be treated as if I did not have a country. I was glad they did not beat us, because even the police there would do nothing to help.

The bus did not return for Ngut, so he walked the hour and a half to Mizan. When he arrived, we found a room at a motel with two beds and paid thirty birr for the night. It was time for dinner, so we went out to find something to eat. In this part of the city, pickpockets infiltrated the streets. They were so smooth that you would not feel when they stole from you. It was important to be always on the lookout and to watch your friends' backs. We made it to the restaurant and back without incident, but we knew they were eying us.

At the motel, I could not fall asleep. I kept thinking about what had happened on the bus. It still bothered me to have been treated so poorly just because I was from a different place. I knew that thinking about it would not change anything. Still, I could not stop myself. I closed my eyes and pulled the blanket over my head, but it could not keep out the sound of the men on the bus laughing at me.

The next morning we discovered that the road to Dimma was too rough for buses. We would have to wait for one of the Isuzu trucks from camp to make the trip. We tried to board the first truck, but it was full, and the driver refused to take us. At least, that's what he said. We had no way of knowing whether it was actually full or if they just did not want to take us. Perhaps they thought we were foreigners.

We kept waiting. Eventually, another truck came by to deliver tires on the way to Dimma. Ngut asked the driver if he would take us to Dimma if we paid him. He charged us forty birr instead of twenty-five birr, the regular fare, but agreed. We had no choice but to pay him the extra amount because staying another night in Mizan would cost even more. Our allowance of 250 birr from IOM was running out, but we made it back to Dimma.

After missing school for two weeks, the time it took to get my medical exam, I was no longer used to walking four miles each way to school. My leg started to hurt, so I went to see a doctor. After examining me, he advised me to stop walking long distances because it aggravated my leg. I followed his instructions and stopped going to school. Now I spent most of my time in the tobacco shop waiting on customers.

The IOM results arrived about two months after the medical examinations and about a year after I first learned I would go to the USA. Lists of names were posted on a board outside of the United Nations compound. My brothers and I were among those who had passed the medical exam and were one step closer to political asylum in the United States. Those who had failed the medical checkup were heartbroken and miserable after coming so far. Now they had no hope for a better life. We were happy to have passed but still apprehensive about the final step before being granted political asylum.

Now we had to wait for the immigration lawyers to finalize our visas and I-94s, which would allow us to legally live and work in the United States. For a while, this was all we talked about in the camp. A better life and opportunities to build a better future were almost within our grasp. Still, we had to wait for the final word from the IOM lawyer to finalize everything. We did not celebrate until the lawyer returned with the final word.

Then I began to hear rumors at the camp that made me worry about the United States. Some people said, "Once you reach the United States, you will never come back." People who had learned about slavery in the United States told us about slaves who were shipped from Africa to Europe and the United States. To scare us even more, they said, "People who refuse to get on the plane will be sedated against their will and forced on." Others said this was an indirect form of slavery. I started to get scared. If I could never come back, I was not sure I still wanted to go to the United States. I was not sure I could live without seeing my parents again. I was confused by what different people were saying.

The wait for our departure was bittersweet. On the one hand, I was grateful for the opportunity to go to the United States, where my leg would be treated and I would have a chance to start a new life and work toward a better future. On the other hand, I was sad to leave my family again, especially since there was no way to say goodbye. I had not heard from my parents since leaving South Sudan two and a half years earlier. Now I was seventeen—and our parents had no idea we were leaving for the United States.

Chapter 16

Miracle Journey

I was going to the United States! Our request for political asylum in the United States had been approved! When new notices were posted on the United Nations board, we found our names on the list. It was final. My crazy daydreams of getting my leg fixed and walking again without crutches suddenly weren't crazy anymore. My hope and long waiting had been rewarded. In fact, we would leave in just five days.

The next four days were spent celebrating and preparing. Some people spent the whole time getting drunk. We were encouraged to give away our clothes because we believed that we would be given money to buy new clothes along the way. I gave my blanket to Gatbel and both my black pants and long-sleeved red shirt to Chuol. I gave a white T-shirt to Changkuoth. I gave everything away to my friends except my jeans, which I happily gave to a relative in Addis Ababa. They all needed clothes more than I did.

The morning of day five, we headed to the United Nations compound, where the whole camp had gathered to see us off, as if everyone was moving out. Those were the happy, smiling faces. The sad faces belonged to those who had not been approved and must stay behind. I thought about my family when I saw others saying goodbye to their loved ones. It was hard to accept that I was leaving them behind. Hardest was not knowing if I would ever see my family again.

A man with a microphone called for everyone's attention and instructed those leaving to stand on the left and all those staying to stand on the right. When he called each head of family, we were supposed to go together to collect the boarding pass for transport in Isuzu mini-vans with no tops or seats; we sat on our bags. After all had boarded and cars began to move, some people walked alongside until the drivers sped up. They vanished in the red dust from the dirt road. I will never forget that ride in 1999, the crowd and the dust that marked the end of my time at the camp and the start of my miracle journey.

Our route over narrow dirt roads to Addis Ababa, Ethiopia's capital city, was one of the most dangerous in the world. The zigzag road twisted around the edge of mountains without so much as a fence to keep us from plunging to our deaths. Drivers had to be extra cautious. Sometimes, they let us off the bus in order to make a turn. That way, if the bus slipped off the cliff, only the driver would go with it.

But God was with us, and two and a half days later, we arrived safely in Addis Ababa. Now, for the first time, I saw buildings ten stories high. We were given money and two days to shop for new, loose clothes because we were likely to gain weight once we reached the United States. It would be awful not to have clothes that fit once we had enough food, so we did as we were told. I purchased a T-shirt two inches too big, a button-down dress shirt with blue, red, and brown stripes, jeans, a belt, and a red-and-black winter jacket. We had been warned that the United States was very cold in winter season.

On the third day, we were taken to the hotel behind the airport to wait for our plane. Three hours before midnight, our expected departure, we were lined up outside the airport, and each family was given a plastic IOM bag with our documents. Ngut also had our tickets and fifty dollars to buy food at the airports. The airport had a lot of glass windows and lights, which made it feel as though it were still day. I wondered if this was how airports in the United States would look. I also wondered if there would be a lot of cars on the streets and ten-story buildings like here in Addis Ababa.

I still could not believe that I had actually left the refugee camp and was now waiting to fly out of Addis Ababa to go to the United States. I hadn't the slightest idea how long a journey this would be.

Finally, at forty-five minutes after midnight, a voice from the ceiling told us to report to the gate because it was time to board the plane. Some people had fallen asleep, but we quickly got up to stand in line. I walked with one crutch down a tiny path in a tunnel and was greeted by the flight attendant, who directed us to our seats. We had expected to walk outside before getting on the plane, so many did not believe that they were actually on a plane until it started to roll away from the terminal. An attendant checked seat belts and told us to sit still. Noises from the engines became louder and louder as we sped down the runway and then tipped up into the air. I sat in a middle row and could not see Africa below us. But I knew. *This is really happening. I am really going to the United States.* A couple of hours later, we stopped in Cairo, Egypt, to pick up more passengers.

On the plane, we were given food we had never seen before. The meats were especially foreign to us. Our main Nuer diet consisted of milk, fish, and corn or sorghum flour. We ate meats only once in a while. After being served clams and shellfish, which are used as bait and not eaten by Nuer, I was grossed out and almost threw up just looking at them. I decided to eat only the foods I recognized, like bread, milk and tea. The flight attendant should have given us the menu with the food pictures, not words, so we could select the kind of food we wanted to eat. Then the clams and shellfish would not have been wasted; other people in the plane would have enjoyed them. We Nuer might be some of the pickiest eaters in the world.

When we landed in Rome for an eight-hour layover, I was sure we would have to walk outside from the plane to the terminal. Once again, however, a tunnel (Jetway) led directly from the plane to the building. After we found our flight to the United States, all we could do was wait. During this time, I noticed people from all over the world carrying IOM bags. Despite the long wait, we did not eat anything. Some people napped, but mostly we just waited. I did not recognize the language the airport workers were speaking, but it was not English. Even though I did not speak English and could only understand through a translator, I knew how it sounded. Maybe I was hearing Italian for the first time.

Finally, a voice using this language announced something. We could not see who was speaking, so I thought she was behind a door. Then another hidden person announced in English: "Be ready to get in line at the gate in five minutes. Please have your passports ready. Thank you."

We joined the line and boarded the plane through a tunnel identical to the one in Addis Ababa. This plane was larger than the one that took us from Ethiopia to Rome, so it took a little longer to find our seats. Slowly, the plane lumbered to the runway for takeoff. A flight attendant announced that this was a nonstop flight to the United States of America.

My seat faced a flat screen that showed a map of the world. I saw our plane moving over a blue area and thought it represented blue sky. Then I got confused. How could the sky be under the plane? Shouldn't the plane be under the sky? Only if we were flying upside down would the sky seem to be under the plane. As dumb as it sounds, I had no geography knowledge whatsoever. I could not even point out the continent of Africa, let alone Sudan, on the world map because I had never seen one. I knew nothing about the Atlantic Ocean.

As we prepared for landing, the flight attendant told us to stay seated, but the more we descended, the scarier it became. Some women screamed every time the plane dropped lower to the ground. I was scared, too. Every time the plane dipped, I felt I was floating above my seat. When we touched down at JFK Airport, everyone clapped with happiness that we had made it safely.

We got off the plane and entered the airport on the second floor through yet another tunnel. *I am in the United States of America!* I said to myself. Now my dream come true presented new challenges. We found that instead of walking down the stairs to the first floor, we were supposed to ride the stairs. I had used regular stairs, but not these. We did not know to get on the escalator quickly with two feet. It must have been funny to watch us who had never ridden an escalator step on with just one foot while the other was left dragging behind. We could not help but laugh at ourselves.

In the airport, we felt that people were staring at us. Maybe they were wondering where we came from. Maybe they were trying to figure out why we were so skinny and thought we were sick or something. Maybe they were curious about our manhood marks, ear to ear across our foreheads.

On the lower level, IOM workers waited to meet us. One lady approached and asked my brother in very Basic English, "Is your name Ngut?" When he said yes, she asked us to follow her along with the family of Nhial, the man standing next to us. People began to go their separate ways as she led us through the glass doors that opened by themselves by magic. *How could that be? Someone must be opening them from the side.* I looked back but could see no one. The doors did open by themselves. What a strange place!

Strange, but beautiful. The lights inside JFK dazzled me. As we made our way to the exit, I saw many more people sitting and walking in the opposite direction. It seemed everyone was in a rush to go somewhere. Then I saw a small car (golf cart) transporting people inside the airport. *Cars are driven even indoors in the United States! Amazing!*

After crossing a very busy street, we boarded the bus to another terminal, where we would catch our final flight to New Hampshire. I pressed my face against the glass window for the entire ride, entranced by my first views of New York City, America. The incredibly tall buildings were unlike anything I had ever seen. No wonder they were called skyscrapers. And just days before, I had thought the ten-story buildings in Addis Ababa were tall. I saw more colors than I could even name in my native language. *So this is America. No wonder so many people want to come here.*

After a couple of hours in the second terminal, the lady who had met us delivered us to our gate. Nhial and his family went to a different gate. We did not know where we were going, and I started to worry about being separated from the other families, the two hundred people on the plane. Now my brothers and I were on our own. I could not help thinking about the frightening things people had warned about back at the camp, like being taken as an indirect slave. Could that be why we were separated? I had thought we would all live close to one another, as we had in Ethiopia. *This cannot be true. This cannot be happening. Now that we are divided, will I be sent to an individual master?* My excitement turned to worry.

Our final flight landed in Manchester, New Hampshire, on May 26, 1999, at 9:00 p.m. I could not see much from the air except lights and streetlights. This city would become my home for the next decade. Representatives from the International Institute, Sarah and a man whose name I cannot remember, picked us up at the airport. The ride revealed a city with small houses and not skyscrapers.

The lady was from North Sudan and spoke Arabic. She explained things like lights, kitchen, and bathroom fixtures—all new to us. Now we would use a toilet, not the bushes. We would use a bathtub and shower, not the river. Our one-bedroom studio apartment was three times bigger than the hut we had shared in Dimma Refugee Camp and had three roll-up beds, one for each of us.

As our hosts left, Sarah told us someone would be by the next day to bring us to the office for paperwork. Exhausted after our long journey, we prepared our beds but fell asleep before even changing into our nightclothes. I do not think I moved one inch all night.

The next morning, I woke to the unreality of my new home. Just a week earlier, I had been in the Dimma Refugee Camp in Ethiopia. Now all doubts had vanished. I was here with my brothers. Never before would I have dreamed of coming to America. The thought would not have entered my mind. It seemed impossible. But not for God. God works in mysterious ways, making the impossible possible. I am living proof because I escaped death and made it to the United States. I am God's living miracle.

Epilogue

Alive for a Reason

Though I have lived in the United States since 1999, my Nuer family tree endures in my mind, and my father's teachings still guide me. In fact, I remember them every day. When I flash back to my Nuer boyhood, I remember our time together and very briefly become a small boy again. I thank him for his teachings and protection. I know beyond doubt that my father lives in me, and I think that he would respect the man I am becoming. Now it is my turn to be protector.

My Mama Jeanne in New Hampshire once said, "God kept you alive for a reason." Telling my story of conscription and injury in Sudan's civil war may be that reason. I speak for the hundreds of thousands of children in South Sudan and elsewhere who are war victims like me, who have no voice and untold histories of trauma, who have no one to protect them.

Children are the number one victims during war. At first, I did not understand what was happening or why. Once I did understand, I worried for my family. *What if I get killed? What if my parents get killed? What will happen to me? To my siblings?* These became recurring nightmares. Despite my crippling wound, I did survive; so did my parents. Other children were not so lucky and became orphans with no one to care for them. Physical injury is just the beginning. All of us witnessed atrocities that have left permanent psychological scars. Nothing will ever erase them. Love and a second chance rescued me. Please advocate for children who are victims of war.

God bless you.

- UNICEF
- Red Cross
- Ascentria Refugee and Immigrant Services

Acknowledgements

I would like to thank the following people from the bottom of my heart for the roles they played in my life.

Thank you, Mama Jeanne, for taking on the role of mother when you recognized I needed one, even as a grown man. I thank you for your unconditional love over the years. Having you in my life has truly been a blessing. Thank you for believing in me and encouraging me to write a book about my childhood. For all of those times I told you, "Maybe someday," I'm glad "someday" has finally come. If it were not for you, I never would have written this book. I will never forget all the times you said to me, "God kept you for alive for a reason, Gatluk." You were the driving force behind me writing this book. Thank you, Mama Jeanne, for always believing in me.

Thank you, Alan and Jeannie Peterson, with all of my heart. Jeannie, you became like a mother to me; Alan, you became like a father. When years ago you told the doctor that your friendship with me was like father and son, I knew you meant it. I thank you for everything you have ever done for me, from finding time to visit me in college to making sure I was keeping up with my schoolwork. When my own dad could not be at my graduation, you were there. Thank you for never turning your back on me, through good times and bad. I am lucky to have you and Jeannie in my life and always making me feel at home.

Three months after my arrival in Manchester, New Hampshire, I began medical treatment to repair my hip and leg, a long and painful journey. After thirteen surgeries, my dream to walk without crutches came true: despite a permanent limp, I can now walk unaided. I am beyond grateful to the medical communities at Concord Hospital and Dr. Michael

Herbenick and Dartmouth-Hitchcock Hospital and Dr. Peter Cook, in particular.

I would like to thank Gail Schilling for her tremendous help with this project. I thank you for believing in me and bringing this project to life. Without your help and encouragement, this book would not have included many important details. Thank you for being patient with me.

As for my mother, the late Nyalam Kun Chol, the backbone of our family, I thank you for being the string that held our family together until you went to your heavenly home in 2016. You were the foundation of our family and my life. I could not even imagine being born to any other woman but you. Your love and care to us during those tough, difficult times, never failed. I love you, Mom!

Last but not least, I thank my late father, Gatluak Digiew Tut, for raising me to be the man I am today. With love, support, and daring, you taught me to love God, respect others, and work hard. You are my hero, and I carry you in my spirit.

Printed in the United States
By Bookmasters